How to Rebuild
SMALL-BLOCK
FORD

GEORGE REID

CarTech®
Auto Books & Manuals

Edited By: Travis Thompson

ISBN-13 978-1-932494-04-4
ISBN-10 1-932494-04-9

Part No. SA102

Printed in China

Title Page: Our 289 is ready to go to work. We have remembered important issues, such as a new radiator, engine mounts, clutch, throwout bearing, water pump, and any other potential weak spots.

Back Cover

Upper Left: A degree wheel is one of those specialty tools you're not always going to need. You can rent a degree wheel and pointer locally.

Upper Right: If we opt for a custom crankshaft with even greater stroke, we can achieve a 3.50-inch stroke, which balloons our 302 into a 355 cubic incher.

Lower Right: Screw-in, adjustable-rocker-arm studs are installed next. Teflon sealer is used on these studs. Torque these studs to 35 ft-lbs. Use Poly-Loc adjustment nuts.

CarTech® Inc.
39966 Grand Avenue
North Branch, MN 55056
Telephone (651) 277-1200 • (800) 551-4754 • Fax: (651) 277-1203
www.cartechbooks.com

OVERSEAS DISTRIBUTION BY:

Brooklands Books Ltd.
P.O. Box 146, Cobham, Surrey, KT11 1LG, England
Telephone 01932 865051 • Fax 01932 868803
www.brooklands-books.com

Brooklands Books Aus.
3/37-39 Green Street, Banksmeadow, NSW 2109, Australia
Telephone 2 9695 7055 • Fax 2 9695 7355

TABLE OF CONTENTS

Workbench Tips

ACKNOWLEDGMENTS

When CarTech® Editor Steve Hendrickson handed me this assignment, I knew the people I could count on for help. Through the years, I've been able to count on a seasoned battery of other authors, writers, historians, automobile restorers, engine builders, and extraordinary friends to help me meet the standards you expect from CarTech® Books.

Jim Smart, Senior Editor at *Mustang Monthly Magazine* and *Mustang & Fords,* has been very instrumental in helping me with numerous CarTech® book projects. John Da Luz, of JMC Motorsports, and Mark Jeffrey, of Trans-Am Racing, have helped me with a variety of book projects. Larry Ofria of Valley Head Service is yet another friend and professional engine builder who has been very helpful to me.

This book project involves a new, yet very seasoned name in the engine building business – Jim Grubbs. Grubbs, a retired Los Angeles Police Department officer, discovered his passion and talent for engine building more than 20 years ago. Instead of fighting crime, he decided to fight substandard engine performance. Jim Grubbs Motorsports was founded as a result of his passion for internal combustion.

Today, JGM builds dozens of engines in a given year, with a proven track record on streets and racetracks from coast to coast. My engine-building experience with Jim Grubbs Motorsports has been very rewarding, and much of what I learned made it into this book.

I'm going to take all this learning experience and pass it along to you in the form of images and words to help you make the most of your engine-building effort. I want to thank all of these wonderful people for their commitment and help on this book project.

—*George Reid*

WHAT IS A WORKBENCH® BOOK?

This is an S-A Design *Workbench®* book. It doesn't present a hasty look at small-block Ford engine building and modification, nor does it give vague advice or only cover the high points. Furthermore, this book doesn't require that you've had previous experience with engine building or a degree in engineering to use it. *This book is a complete reference that shows you how to rebuild a small-block Ford; step-by-step, every step, with nothing left out!* Hundreds of photos guide you through the easy and "tricky" procedures, and photo captions explain exactly where to look for possible problems and how to fix them. This book shows you how to rebuild your engine and ensure that it's working perfectly.

However, this book is more than a "rebuild" manual. The authors and the editors at S-A Design have packed this book with information about components and accessories, including a wide range of performance tips and modification procedures to improve power and economy – and we didn't stop there. We wanted you to get the same professional results on your first rebuild that the pros get after years of experience. So we've detailed the special components, tools, chemicals, and other accessories you'll need to get the job done right, *the first time.* You'll even find tips that will save

you money without compromising "top-notch" results. To round things out, we've included a *Work-A-long Sheet®* to help you record vital statistics while you work on your engine.

This book isn't meant to replace other books on your bookshelf. (In fact, if you're looking for in-depth information on performance modifications or racing tips, refer to any one of several best-selling S-A Design books, including *Engine Blueprinting, How to Build Max Performance Ford V-8s on a Budget, How to Build Big-Inch Ford Small Blocks, Street Supercharging, and How to Install and Use Nitrous Oxide.* Look inside the front and back covers for ordering information.) The book you're holding is meant to detail, like never before, the "workbench" procedures required to rebuild and assemble your engine – using the same tried and true techniques used by hundreds of professional engine builders – and prepare the finished engine for optimum street or strip performance. If these are your goals, you've got the right book.

WHY THIS BOOK IS DIFFERENT

While virtually every other performance book is a series of "typical-looking" chapters, this *Workbench®* book is quite different. Why did we

make it different? The answer is simple: We had to! This book not only helps you become familiar with small-block Ford engines and the tools and materials you need to work on them, it also shows how to rebuild an engine in your own workshop, step-by-step. This means that it must look different from other books. It must have hundreds of photos (more than 500!) to guide you through the entire rebuilding process. This book also illustrates many of the performance components, accessories, and upgrades that have been developed for the small-block Ford engine. This additional information is easy to find and clearly separated from the step-by-step sequences. Through the use of "*Workbench® Tips,*" icon-labeled photos, and extensive cross-references, this book presents both stock and performance information and keeps each separate and accessible.

TEXT AND PHOTO CHAPTERS

The text and photo sections are the familiar part of this book. They consist of columns of text combined with photos, drawings, and charts. These familiar-looking pages contain the basic information you'll need to obtain the proper tools and accessories to begin specific building procedures.

MASTER MECHANIC

 Ignition timing is set two ways. At idle, timing should be dialed in around 12 degree BTDC. Total advance should be no higher than 36 degrees BTDC. During our dyno pull, Jim Grubbs was able to get the maximum amount of horsepower and torque at 34 degrees BTDC.

This is an example of the hundreds of step-by-step photos in this book. The photos will guide you through the easy and "tricky" procedures, while the captions explain exactly what to do, what not to do, and how to avoid possible problems.

Conventional text and photos are the traditional and most familiar way to present information about these wide-ranging topics. However, the best way to show the detailed procedures involved in rebuilding an engine is to show how *with step-by-step photos.*

STEP-BY-STEP PHOTOS AND ICONS

Each of the step-by-step photo sections include a sequence of numbered photos and captions that illustrate virtually every operation involved in rebuilding a typical small-block Ford engine for general street or high-performance use.

As we mentioned, the goal of this book is more than just rebuilding a stock engine. The step-by-step chapters also include many additional photos that show how to install performance or heavy-duty components, how to modify stock components for special applications, or even call attention to assembly steps that are critical to proper operation or safety. To keep these photos separated from the main rebuild sequence, we have labeled them with unique "icons." These symbols represent an idea, and photos marked with icons contain important, specialized information. An icon-labeled step may apply to your engine, in which case you should include the step in your rebuild. On the other hand, it may illustrate a modification that doesn't apply to your specific application; in this case, just skip it and continue with the next photo in the sequence.

Here are some of the icons found in S-A Design *Workbench* books:

 TORQUING FASTENERS – Illustrates a fastener that must be properly tightened with a torque wrench at this point in the rebuild. The torque specs are usually provided in the step.

 SPECIAL TOOL USED – Illustrates the use of a special tool that may be required or can make the job easier (caption with photo will explain further).

 PRECISION MEASUREMENT – Illustrates a precision measurement or adjustment that is required at this point in the rebuild.

! **IMPORTANT! –** Photo indicates a step in the rebuild that is very important for the correct assembly or preparation of components.

 SAFETY STEP – Indicates a step in the rebuild that is essential for the safe operation of the engine or to guard the personal safety of the rebuilder.

 CRITICAL INSPECTION – Indicates that a component must be inspected to ensure proper operation of the engine.

 PERFORMANCE TIP – Indicates a procedure that applies to only high-performance or racing engines, or details a modification that can improve performance.

 ECONOMY STEP – Indicates an optional modification or procedure that may improve engine efficiency and fuel economy.

 MASTER MECHANIC TIP – Illustrates a step in the rebuild that non-professionals may not know. It may illustrate a shortcut, or a trick to improve reliability, prevent component damage, etc.

 NOTATION REQUIRED – Illustrates a point in the rebuild where the reader should write down a particular measurement, size, part number, etc., for later reference.

 SAVE MONEY – Illustrates a method or alternate method of performing a rebuild step that will save money but still give acceptable results.

The step-by-step photo chapters may include optional steps labeled with icons. This book also includes other optional information that, although it may not be essential for building a specific engine, the reader may find useful. These optional information "packages" are called *Workbench Tips*, and they can be found throughout the book.

Workbench® Tips

This book contains *Workbench Tips*. They're easy to spot; look for a box with the *"Workbench Tip"* label at the top containing a group of photos and some text. These tips cover subjects that are generally too short for the text-and-photo chapters but present more information than a single icon-labeled photo. The author and editors selected topics that they felt would be interesting and valuable. Many contain hints that a professional may have discovered after years of work. For example, there are *Workbench Tips* on how to restore damaged threads, how to use precision tools, upgrading engine components, sources for unique or special parts, and much more.

The *Workbench Tips* are not presented in a specific order. However, you'll find a complete subject list in the *Workbench Tips* table of contents on page 4. You can read the *Workbench Tips* one at a time as you progress through the book, you can look up specific *Workbench Tips* at any time, or you can even skip everything else and just read the *Workbench Tips*. However you choose to use *Workbench Tip* information, we hope it will add to your understanding of the small-block Ford and help you get the most power, economy, and reliability from your engine.

Where to Begin

How to Rebuild the Small-Block Ford is organized in a sequence that, theoretically, allows you to start at the first chapter and read straight through to the end. When you're finished, you should have a top-quality rebuilt engine. However, one reader may want to focus on the final assembly information in Chapter 5, while another may want information about a performance accessory described in a *Workbench Tip*, and others may be interested in the advice on the tools required for rebuilding, found in Chapter 1. Because of these wide-ranging needs, here are some tips for using this book:

If you're starting from scratch to rebuild a street engine: Start with Chapter 1 and read the whole book, in order.

If you have some experience and would like to assemble an engine from miscellaneous components: Start with Chapter 4 and review important issues that you need to discuss with your machine shop, then continue through the remainder of the book.

If you want to study and learn how to calculate your exact compression ratio based on measurements you've taken: Jump to Chapter 8: Engine Math. You might be surprised how little changes can add up to a lot more or less compression than you thought you'd have.

For all readers: Review the Tables of Contents and study any unfamiliar information, until it makes sense. Carefully review and study the entire rebuild sequence before you begin your project. The more you understand and practice these techniques, the more you'll benefit from – and enjoy – precision engine building.

Several other S-A Design books contain information that you may find very useful in your engine building project. Some of these books are pictured or mentioned here. If you would like a complete catalog of S-A Design publications, visit our website at www.cartechbooks.com, or call us toll-free at 800-551-4754.

BEFORE YOU BEGIN

Building an engine is a golden opportunity to know exactly what's inside. Think of your engine as a blank canvass, ready for liberal doses of oil, paint, and creativity.

Rebuilding an engine can be a very rewarding experience. It's a golden opportunity to start anew, with fresh components and perfectly machined surfaces married together in blissful harmony. When you build an engine, you become familiar with what the engine is. There is no wondering here – you know exactly what you have under the hood. You can start an educated performance tuning and maintenance program that will allow your new engine to live for a long time. Contrary to the old 100,000-mile (or less) theory of engine life, well-built engines can live 200,000 to 300,000 miles with regular preventative maintenance and a civilized driving technique.

Why do engines live longer today than they did years ago? Much of the improvement is centered around better lubrication technology, lead-free gasoline,

electronic engine control, overdrive transmissions, and a host of other elements that make life easier on the engine. Likely the single greatest benefit for engines today is unleaded gasoline. In the 1980s, car buffs were very concerned over the loss of lead in gasoline. There was fear that unleaded fuels would harm valve seats and cause premature engine failure. The valve seat part is certainly true. If you drive a car everyday using unleaded fuel and iron valve seats, it will wind up needing a valve job. Big deal. That is the only sacrifice you'll have to make using unleaded gasoline. The benefits are far more numerous – a cleaner engine, cleaner air, longer exhaust system life, and certainly longer engine life.

Engines also live longer because companies like Mobil have developed synthetic lubricants that offer excellent staying power, longer service life, and cleaner operation. If you run Mobil 1 in your small-block Ford, change it with great regularity every 5,000 miles, and use a Wix or Motorcraft oil filter, you can achieve 200,000 to 300,000 miles on a rebuild. We offer no guarantees because every engine, and every driver, is different. If you run your engine hard, it won't live as long. If you consistently forget to change the oil, it won't live as long. If you let it get out of tune, it may not live as long.

To build an engine that will serve you for thousands of miles, you have to know

what you have to begin with. All the best machining technique and highest-quality parts are worthless if you have a flawed casting or forging that will fail when the engine is fired up. This is why the teardown is as critical as the build up.

Before you can begin on your engine project, you have to be committed to what you want the engine to do, and be willing to stick with that plan. What's the most severe treatment you intend to throw at this engine? How will you use this engine most of the time? And, the most important question – how much do you have to spend? How you intend to

When an engine arrives at the machine shop, there are many unknowns that become discoveries as we knock the engine apart. We would quickly learn we needed a block, new valves and guides, and more.

use the engine is directly affected by how much you have to spend. Tight budgets call for a whole lot of common sense, which means knowing how to make the most of your money.

Building a small-block Ford costs anywhere from $1,200 to $15,000, depending on your expectations. A mild-mannered, easy-to-live-with small-block Ford you're going to use everyday can be achieved for $1,200 if you do most of the work yourself. And, if you take good care of it, including the use of Mobil 1 synthetic engine oil, you can easily achieve between 100,000 and 200,000 miles. If you expect to spin it to 9,000 rpm on a road-race course, circle track, or drag strip, you can expect to spend $15,000 in parts and labor. How much do you have in the checking account? More importantly, how much engine do you actually need?

We are all guilty of bench-racing ego, and many of us build way more engine than we actually need. It sounds so good during a boast fest with your buddies. We all like to talk up our engine build plans. But why spend more money on an engine than you have to, especially if you're going to build it for the daily commute or weekend cruising? Pleasure cruisers don't

Engine building projects begin all sorts of ways. Sometimes, we stumble upon an engine like this one, with no idea of its condition internally. The problem here is whether or not we have found an engine that has already been rebuilt. Rebuilt engines that are worn out typically have 4.030-inch bores. Small-block Fords can be bored out to 4.040 inches, but we discourage a 4.060-inch bore size. It's always a gamble until you remove the cylinder head and measure the bores.

need H-beam connecting rods, steel cranks, and forged pistons. And they don't really need aftermarket cylinder heads with expensive port work, either. They need the very basics of what Ford provid-

ed in the beginning, plus improvements that will make them peppy, reliable engines they can count on for years to come.

Daily drivers and weekend cruisers need only have the small-block they had to begin with, plus reliability improvements like hardened exhaust valve seats, high-volume oil pumps, roller camshafts, high-performance valve seals, bronze valveguides (or replacement of the valveguides entirely), new valves, high-tech gaskets and seals, hypereutectic pistons, electronic ignition, and more. Your goal with a mild street engine is to make it as reliable as you can make it while pumping up the power a bit.

CRITICAL INSPECTION

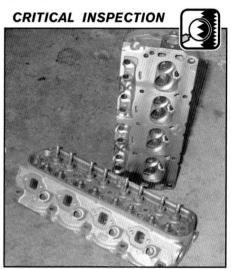

 Engine building projects are best started with hand-picked castings and forgings. Look to mass engine builders and parts houses for castings. Always opt for a matched set of heads and block, meaning the same casting numbers and similar date codes.

If you intend to do some weekend drag racing, you need to decide how fast you want the vehicle to be and what you can afford. The quarter-mile times you are seeking are directly proportional to what you have to spend. Racing engines take a lot of effective planning and a realistic approach. In the racing world, there is no such thing as compromise. You have to be prepared to spend wisely and go after the best bang for the buck. Cutting corners with a racing engine is foolish. If you try to save a few bucks, you could wind up spending a fortune later when the darned thing

Build for the Mission
WORKBENCH TIP

If you want to save a whole lot of money, plan your engine realistically and don't overbuild. Engines for the daily commute don't need steel cranks, H-beam rods, and forged pistons. They don't need an 850-cfm carburetor either. Plan your engine for exactly the driving you intend to do – and leave the bench racing and boasting for the dreamers down at the drive-in.

Engines built for daily commuters, for example, don't need pure-race technology inside. They need to be planned and built for reliability and economy. This doesn't mean you have to sacrifice power. Using a nodular-iron crankshaft, heavy-duty I-beam rods, and hypereutectic pistons nets you reliability and

performance. If you want an aggressive camshaft that will give you power, seriously consider a roller hydraulic camshaft with .500-inch lift or less. Go for duration and good valve overlap. A high-lift camshaft (above .500-inch) will beat the daylights out of your engine's valves and springs – which hurts reliability. For more on choosing a cam, check out Chapter 3.

Performance and reliability are always about compromise. To get reliability, you have to give away some performance. To get a lot of performance, you have to give up a certain amount of reliability. It's always a tradeoff. It is up to you to determine how far to go in either direction.

blows up. You have to think of a racing engine like you would an aircraft engine. There's no compromising with an aircraft engine – because airplanes can't just pull over and call a tow truck. When racing engines fail, like aircraft engines, they typically fail catastrophically. So let's dive right in with realistic expectations about budget and limitations.

Engine building should always begin with a mental blueprint of how your engine is going to be built. Are you going to collect the castings and parts yourself *and* build the engine? Are you going to begin with a manufactured short-block or long-block? Are you going to opt for an engine kit? How you approach your engine build beforehand determines the outcome. Crate short- and long-blocks are an excellent choice that can save you a lot of money if you know and trust the builder. Regardless of who the builder is, all crate engines must be checked in great detail before you install them in the vehicle.

Any time you can buy a crate engine for $800 to $1,200, you're not going to get the same value you would from an engine built from the ground up at a local machine shop. Buying a low-buck crate engine means really cheap cast pistons, rings, bearings, and the like. It can even mean .030-inch oversize pistons in some bores, with .040- or .060-inch oversize pistons in others. We've seen this enough times to know it is a matter of practice with the low-buck engine builders. They cannot afford to lose the value of a single core block. So, they fudge the rules a bit, taking some bores to 4.040 and 4.060 inches in order to save a block that should otherwise be scrapped. This means variations in compression ratio from bore to bore that most people probably wouldn't notice. But, it is something you need to be mindful of during your engine build planning. Don't waste your money on an engine built this way. All bores must be uniform in size without exception. Bearing sizes may also vary too, which certainly isn't as critical as bore size. For example, .010-inch oversize on rods and .020-inch oversize on the mains is not a big deal.

Another important question for the budget mass-production rebuilder is, do they dynamic balance the bottom end? Not all builders do. Dynamic balancing

is critical to smooth operation. The automakers and mass-production engine builders do dynamic balancing to some degree. Pistons, rods, and crankshafts are weight-matched to get them as close to specs as possible. Pistons must weigh within a reasonable amount of each other. So must connecting rods. But this really isn't dynamic balancing. It's a crapshoot with your time and money. We like pain-staking dynamic balancing – with pistons and connecting rods that are precision balanced and adjusted for uniformity. We want piston and rod assemblies that weigh exactly the same as the crankshaft counterweights and flywheel counterweighting. Any irregularities in balancing can induce unhealthy vibration. You may not even feel that vibration. But, your engine will. Vibration is destructive and will bleed life right out of your engine.

While we're on the subject of vibration, it's important to remember there are two types of offset balance with small-block Fords. Small-block Fords are externally balanced, which means we have to balance the flywheel and harmonic balancer to the crank, rods, and pistons. They should not be balanced separately. Small-block Fords built prior to 1982 have a 28-ounce offset balance dialed into the flywheel (manual transmission) or the flexplate (automatic transmission). When Ford came out with the 5.0L High Output V-8 in 1982, this offset balance went to 50 ounces, due to heavier connecting rods and pistons. The 50-ounce spec has been the standard ever since.

If you're having a hard time understanding this 28- and 50-ounce offset issue, you aren't alone. In the old days, the 289 High-Performance V-8 had a slide-on counterweight that went on the nose of the crankshaft. This counterweight offset the additional weight imposed by larger 3/8-inch connecting rod bolts. The same can be said for the 428 Super Cobra Jet, which also had a counterweight to offset heavier connecting rods and bolts. The Boss 302 had this extra weight incorporated into the wider harmonic balancer. Beginning in 1982, Ford infused this added weight into the flywheel/flexplate to offset the even heavier connecting rods and bolts.

Where this 28- versus 50-ounce offset issue becomes challenging is when you're shopping for bottom-end engine parts. Your small-block Ford must have the proper offset balance to keep vibration in check. This means you need a 28-ounce offset flywheel or flexplate if you are building a pre-1982 302. To do this right, you have to know what combination of parts you have. Keep in mind that your machine shop can balance your rotating assembly to 28- or 50-ounce. The choice is yours. Just make sure you know which it is when it is time to buy a flywheel/flexplate and harmonic balancer. A 28-ounce offset flywheel on a 50-ounce offset engine will set up an ugly vibration.

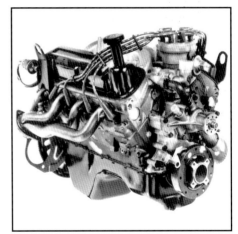

Crate engines can be a good value if you know what's inside them. Not all crate engines are created equal. If you are considering the $800 short-block from a discount auto parts store, carefully consider this decision. If you're building a rarely driven show car, low-buck short-blocks and long-blocks might be a good value. If you're building a driver, opt for something better. Don't be fooled by nameplates. Just because it is a Ford remanufactured engine does not mean it is any better than the $800 to $1,200 discount mill. Verify what's inside first.

The same is true for a 50-ounce flywheel on a 28-ounce engine. Make sure you have a cohesive package.

On top, it's important to understand what kind of valve work you are getting for the money. Are you getting 16 new valves with hardened exhaust valve seats? Or are you getting valves grabbed from a huge barrel with hundreds of other used valves? Are you getting new valveguides or are you getting bronze guides? Are they knurled? Or did the builder forget all about the valveguides and cheat with just a fresh set of seals? These are important questions to ask the budget crate engine builder. Rarely driven show cars don't need hardened exhaust valve seats, but aggressively driven engines need hardened exhaust valve seats, new valves, and guides.

Low-buck budget engines you can buy from national auto parts discounters are not going to be up to the standards you might be expecting. Based on our experiences with remanufactured engines, a lot depends on what you have to spend and how you intend to drive the vehicle. The occasional weekend driver or trailered show car can get away with a low-buck budget engine from AutoZone, Kragen, or Pep Boys, unless you're date-code and casting-number conscious.

If you don't care about date coding or having the correct castings, the discount store crate engine is a nice deal for under $1,500. These crate engines are built by outside contractors, but the same is true for Ford Authorized Remanufactured engines. If you buy a Ford Remanufactured engine through your local Ford dealer or classic car parts house, you are getting the same kind of engine sold through AutoZone, Kragen, CarQuest, or Pep Boys. Ford's standards may be higher, but not by much. You're getting the same kind of warranty – about 90 days to 12 months – depending on the company.

Of all the crate engines and kits we're familiar with, we like the engine kits you can order from Performance Automotive Warehouse and Coast High Performance. Engine kits enable you to see what you are getting before the mill goes together. When it's already assembled, you have no idea what's in there. Both Coast High Performance and Performance Automotive

Warehouse give you the best parts available in their engine kits. Of the two, Performance Automotive Warehouse offers the greatest value for the money because it sells so many of these engines and kits.

Where these engine kits (and all others) need close scrutiny is in the area of machine work. It doesn't hurt to check the new parts when they come out of the boxes. All components should be thoroughly examined by a qualified machinist that you trust. Cylinder bores, line-bores, decks, and the like need to be checked prior to assembly. Disassemble a cylinder head one valve at a time and inspect the seats and guides.

You should do this because mistakes do happen with even the best manufacturers and distributors. These days, mistakes happen with greater frequency because the marketplace has become very competitive. Manufacturers are under great pressure to build these engines and kits for less money. As a result, flawed parts slip through unnoticed. So does sloppy machine work because it is all about volume – and profit. We have seen camshafts that don't match the cam card (mispackaging or poor manufacturing technique). And, we have seen remanufactured blocks with mis-sized pistons and bearings. These mistakes can cost you plenty if they escape unnoticed. It's important for you to discover them before the engine is assembled and installed in the vehicle. The manufacturer's warranty covers replacement of the engine. But, it typically does not cover labor. Install a defective engine and you're out at least the cost of the installation and removal.

With all of these things in mind, which should you choose? Choice boils down to three basic issues – budget, trust, and mission. If you have a tight budget, the humble crate engine isn't a bad deal if you do your homework going in. Homework is a pain in the neck because it is time consuming. Who has time for research today? However, how can you afford not to?

With crate engines, you need to inspect some examples of what you intend to buy from a builder. Talk with reputable local auto repair shops and ask them who sells the best crate engines. These folks don't have time to mess

around with customer jobs that are going to blow up and have to be replaced on their time. The best auto repair shops go with what works and they stay away from what doesn't. Each failed engine for them is lost revenue. Most auto repair shops we've dealt with that service Fords opt for the Ford Remanufactured engines because they offer the best warranty and employ the best parts.

Crate engines and kits are the easy ticket to completion, but there's a great sense of self-satisfaction that comes from building your own engine. Look to a seasoned, qualified machine shop to do your machine work. See to it that everything is properly measured – twice – just to make sure.

You might be tempted to ask – define good parts. Today's crate engine market consists of a lot of off-shore parts where the point of origin is unknown. If it is known, we're not always sure about the quality. We typically have to inspect these parts and make a judgment call one piece at a time. This is where you need to have some faith in American auto parts suppliers and the countries they deal with around the globe. Most of the parts coming out of China are pretty darned good, and often of better quality than you get in the U.S. Pieces coming out of Taiwan and India can be hit and miss.

Companies like Federal-Mogul (Speed Pro, Sealed Power, Fel-Pro) maintain a very high standard with their parts, which means you can count on great consistency time and time again. With Federal-Mogul parts, we've seen packaging from places

Ford Crate Engines

WORKBENCH TIP

If you're thinking seriously about a crate engine, wouldn't it be nice to have a genuine article – a Ford Racing crate engine? It's a popular misconception that you have to order these engines and parts directly from Ford Racing Performance Parts, but this isn't true. There are a lot of vendors, like Mustangs Plus, that offer these engines and parts. A place like Mustangs Plus can give you something Ford Racing does not – a familiar voice and great customer service.

Complete crate engines from Ford Racing Performance Parts are available from places like Mustangs Plus. This is a complete 5.0L High Output engine assembly, shown here panned for a vintage Ford. You can easily change over to a double-sump pan for your Fox-body Mustang.

SAVE MONEY $

$ *If you want to save a few bucks, opt for a pre-built short-block or long-block assembly. The nice thing about these short- and long-block assemblies is convenience. All you need to do is check tolerances before assembling the entire engine.*

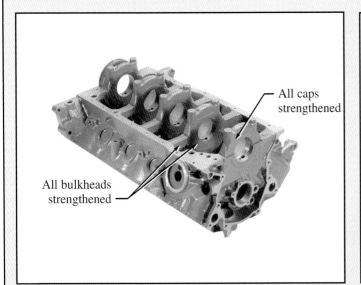

All caps strengthened

All bulkheads strengthened

This is Ford Racing's B50 block. Note the improvements that make it a solid investment. Fit a stroker kit inside this block and go Chevy hunting. This is a good universal block you can do anything with.

The Ford Racing R302 block would be overkill for a street application. However, it is perfect for racing. Note the four-bolt main caps and heavier webbing, just for starters, in this industrial-strength block.

like South Africa, Mexico, and South America, and the quality has been second to none. And that's all we really need to be concerned about in our engine projects.

Engine kits need the same kind of attention as crate engines. We need to inspect them piece by piece, measuring each of the parts before assembly begins. This is just good common sense that will ultimately save you a lot of time and money if there is a problem.

Engine kits typically include a machined block, reworked cylinder heads or new heads, and a complete bottom-end assembly that includes fully machined and dynamic-balanced crankshaft, reconditioned connecting rods, bears and rings, and new forged pistons. Not many engine kits include cast or hypereutectic pistons. Even the most "budget" engine kits from Performance Automotive Warehouse include forged pistons. If you want hypereutectic or cast pistons, you will have to specify when you order the kit. But, don't expect a big price break when you do. Forged pistons are a good deal.

Engine kits typically include everything you need to build either a long- or short-block – including a complete gasket set, camshaft, lifters, rocker arms, pushrods, freeze plugs, oil pump, and a timing set. Engine kits typically do not include fasteners, valve covers, intake manifold, carburetor or fuel injection, ignition system, senders and sensors, spark plugs, alternator, power steering pump, and other bolt-on accessories. These will cost you extra.

PLANNING YOUR ENGINE

Engine planning begins with knowing the path you intend to take. We've already discussed crate engines and kits. Now, we want to address planning and building an engine from scratch. This road is usually for the more experienced engine builder, but you didn't buy this book to take the easy way out.

There are two basic approaches to a from-scratch engine build. The purist method involves using all of the correct date-coded parts, with model-year specific casting numbers. The other is the devil-may-care method, where you use any combination of parts and castings as long as they all work well together.

Ideally, you'll find a small-block Ford that has never been apart. An engine that has never been apart will have standard 4.000-inch bores and will be ready to grow a little. If you get lucky and find a standard-bore block with less than .011-inch of bore taper, you won't have to over-bore it; just hone the block and install standard pistons. This means greater block life, because you can always over-bore it down the road.

So how do you tell if an engine has ever been apart? As a rule, it boils down to the paint and condition of the gaskets and hardware you can see. Ford usually did a nice, clean job of gasket installation, with a minimum of sealer and goop around the edges. Engines that have never been disturbed have virgin paint on their bolt heads. Undisturbed engines have a clean, uncluttered look, even though they may be dirty and greasy. One exception to this rule is engines that have had repair work performed, such as timing set replacements, new oil pumps, rear main seal replacement, gasket replacement, valve jobs, and the like.

The best way to determine an engine's virginity is to pull a cylinder head and measure the bores. A 4.000-inch bore indicates an undisturbed engine. Our project engine for this book, a 1965 289-ci engine, was torn down and rebuilt with high-performance parts back in the 1960s when it was new. Because the bores were nice and true at the time, the builder opted for finish honing and a fresh set of TRW forged aluminum pistons. The original Ford cast pistons were gone.

Our 289-ci block find was a huge exception to the rule. Most small-block Fords, especially older 221s, 260s, 289s,

It isn't as critical to have matching numbers with late-model 5.0L engines because they aren't as collectible as vintage Fords at this time. When we say matching numbers, we're talking an original engine in an original vehicle. Casting and part numbers are what matter because you want to have the right attachment points for all your accessories.

and 302s, have been rebuilt at some time, leaving most of them with .020- and .030-inch oversize bores, making it hard to find rebuildable cores today. Perseverance is the key to finding a rebuildable block. If you are unable to find a rebuildable used block, you may order a new 5.0L or 5.8L bare block from Mustangs Plus. These are all-new Ford castings from Ford Racing Performance Parts. If you go with a new block, you'll need a compatible crankshaft designed for the one-piece rear main seal. This pretty much rules out the older 289/302/351W cranks with the seal lip. Any competent machinist can remove the lip, but we suggest finding a compatible crank to begin with – less time and money involved that way.

Cylinder heads, unless they're cracked or have been milled excessively, are nearly always salvageable. Valveguides and seats can always be replaced. Ford cylinder heads weren't fitted with hardened exhaust valve seats until the early 1970s, which means virtually every Ford cylinder head you're going to find prior to that period will have iron seats.

Whenever you shop for a core engine to build, you want to determine if it has ever been apart. Engines that have been apart typically look like it – gasket sealer weeping out from around the gaskets, chipped paint on bolt heads, and the like. An engine like that can often be a crapshoot depending on how it was rebuilt.

Jim Grubbs Motorsports came to the conclusion that our 289 had already been apart, based on gasket condition, chipped paint, the fact that it was Ford Blue (a '65 engine should be black), brass freeze plugs, the wrong timing cover, and more.

This is our 289-ci V-8 engine project for this book. At first glance, it looks like it has seen better times. It has a loud knock, steam in the exhaust, and is down on power.

Close inspection shows why we think this engine has been apart. It's a '65 Ford casting painted Ford Blue, which is a 1966-up characteristic. It has brass freeze plugs. Factory freeze plugs were steel. Note the gasket sealer seeping from between the castings. We also observed one cylinder-head gasket that was installed backwards, which really made this engine prone to overheating.

When we removed the valve covers from this apparently ill 289, it looked clean inside. It's had plenty of oil changes, and it's void of the sludge we usually see. When you are shopping for a core, this is an important issue.

Usable crankshafts, especially the older 1M cranks with a 2.87-inch stroke for the 221-, 260-, and 289-ci V-8s, are becoming harder to find. This crank was produced from 1962 to '68. The same can be said for the C3AE connecting rod forgings also used in these early Ford small-blocks. If you're not fussy about what's inside your small-block Ford, we suggest searching for what's plentiful and invisible once inside the block. The 302's C8OE rods, 2M crankshaft (3.00-inch stroke), and block are all plentiful and cheap, making a 302-inch small-block even more affordable to build.

Finding a good, rebuildable core takes time scouting the salvage yards, checking the classifieds, visiting eBay, wandering the Internet, and putting the word out for what you need. We have so many means today at our disposal for finding good, rebuildable engines, but it gets challenging when we become very specific about what we want. For example, if you are restoring a '66 Mustang convertible and want to show it as a concours restoration, you are greatly limited to date-code specific castings for the engine build. Date codes and casting numbers are critical to concours restorations and the scrutiny of

show judges. They are also crucial to resale value, especially if you are restoring a 289 High Performance GT or Boss 302.

OUR ENGINE

Jeff Fischbach currently owns a '65 Mustang convertible that belonged to his uncle, who purchased the car new. Jeff's uncle passed away, but Jeff never forgot the meaning behind the special Mustang he inherited. The Mustang's original 289-2V engine had been overhauled once already, with a .040-inch overbore and one damaged cylinder. It was not a rebuildable core unless Jeff was willing to undergo the expense of installing new cylinder sleeves – at $100 a bore. Unless having the original, matching number block matters to you, sleeving a block is unnecessary and expensive. Jeff opted to search for a like replacement. Nothing short of a C5AE block would do, but finding a block with the correct date code would be especially challenging.

Finding these elusive castings is a great challenge because so many of them are gone now, which also makes them expensive. We ended up finding our C5AE short-block for Jeff's Mustang at Mustangs

Etc. in Southern California. Our search of Mustangs Etc.'s engine inventory yielded all kinds of small-block Ford short- and long-blocks. When we eyed the C5AE block (1965 vintage) and the letters "STD" written in the side of the block, we knew we had found just the engine for our '65 Mustang convertible project. It was date-coded in mid 1965, which put it in the vicinity of the Mustang's assembly date code in March. Garrett Marks, of Mustangs Etc., wheeled it out for us on a hand truck. We took it to Jim Grubbs Motorsports in Valencia, California, for the teardown and build up.

We got lucky, and Jeff hit pay dirt. The standard-bore C5AE block came filled with period speed pieces from the 1960s – TRW forged pistons, a radical flat-tappet camshaft, and more. Unfortunately, none of these speed parts made sense for what Jeff wanted to do – to build a stock, 225-horse 289-4V engine for the car his uncle loved so much. We are going to get started on his engine in Chapter 2.

HORSEPOWER AND TORQUE

When you're planning your rebuild and deciding what kind of engine you want in the end, it's important that you

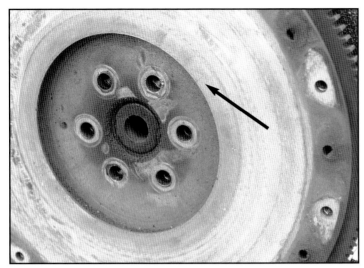

This flywheel suffers from heat damage. Note the heat cracks across the clutch face. It will need to be refaced in order to give the clutch disc a smooth surface to mate with.

Another clue that this engine has been apart: a replacement timing cover with the bolt-on pointer. Original 1962 to '67 small-block Fords have the timing pointer cast into the timing cover.

When an engine fails, we need to understand why. Here's a clue. Look at the scoring the water pump impeller put in the timing cover. The water pump didn't have the separator plate installed, which caused the impeller to score the timing cover. Without the separator plate, the water pump was virtually useless.

think about performance in general, especially the difference between horsepower and torque. We've long been told horsepower is what building an engine is all about. But horsepower is rooted more in Madison Avenue advertising rhetoric than fact. In the power picture, horsepower doesn't count for much. What counts is torque and when we have the most of it. This is especially true when rebuilding an engine to stock or near-stock condition. If it isn't a racecar, don't get hung up building a lot of peak horsepower. Fact: engines make

torque (twist) when we feed fuel and air into combustion chambers and squeeze the mix. John Baechtel of Westech Performance in Ontario, California, said it best when he said, "Torque is the grunt that gets us going, and horsepower is the force that keeps us moving…"

When we look at torque alone, it is the true measure of an engine's work. Horsepower is a measure of how quickly the engine does the work. Torque comes from displacement and stroke mostly. This means the real power we derive from an engine comes in the torque curve. The

broader the torque curve, the better our power package. A broader torque curve comes from making the most of the fuel/air mixture across a broader RPM range. This is best accomplished with a longer stroke and a larger bore. However, our engines need to be planned and built around how we're going to use them. What we choose when it comes to a camshaft, cylinder heads, and induction system determines how our engine will perform and where it will make the greatest torque.

There are plenty of myths about making power, especially in the Ford camp. Bench racers tell us it's easier to make power with a Chevrolet than a Ford. But this just isn't true. You can make just as much power with a Ford for the same amount of money you can a Chevrolet. What gives the Chevrolet an advantage is numbers. Chevrolets are more commonplace than Ford. But this is changing, because Ford's popularity has grown dramatically in recent years. When it comes to seat-of-the-pants performance, there's no black magic here, just the simple physics of taking thermal expansion and turning it into rotary motion that makes power.

To learn how to make power, we have to understand how power is made to begin with inside an engine. How much power an engine makes depends on how much air and fuel we can pump through the engine, plus what we do

Another clue about this engine's history is valvestem length. Here is the correct valvestem tip length for a 1962 through early 1966 221/260/289 engine.

This is the longer mid-1966 and up valvestem tip for rail-style rocker arms, which first came on-line May 8, 1966. This is not the correct valvestem for our 1965-vintage engine. This is your first clue about budget crate engines. This one was a Heinz 57 variety pack – it wasn't a good bargain because it didn't live very long – too many incompatible parts.

with that fuel and air mixture during that split-second it lives and dies in the combustion chambers.

We have to think of an internal combustion engine as an air pump. The more air and fuel we can huff through the cylinders, the more power we're going to make. This is why racers use big carburetors, manifolds, heads, superchargers, turbochargers, and nitrous oxide. Racers know this air-pump theory and practice it with reckless abandon, but this isn't the case for general rebuilds. Street engines for the daily commute need to be planned for good low- and mid-range torque. Drag racing engines need to make power at mid to high RPM. Road racing engines need to be able to do it all – down low, in the middle, and at high RPM, because they're going to live in all of these ranges while racing. Engines scheduled for trailer towing need plenty of low-end torque. They also need to be able to live comfortably at mid-range, when we're going to be pulling a grade.

Engines have to be planned and executed for the mission or you're bound to be disappointed. We've all seen the radical engine in a street car that won't idle, which falls on its face when the traffic light turns green. This is an engine that is happiest when it is spinning at 6,000 rpm. Great for

the racetrack – lousy for the street. This is where you have to be disciplined in your planning, and build an engine that's well suited to your intended use.

TOOLS TO GET THE JOB DONE

When you're building engines, it is easy to become overwhelmed with tool and equipment issues. It's also easy to go crazy with the credit card. That first trip to Sears or Harbor Freight is often like that first trip to the speed shop. You lay down the plastic and come home with a lot of stuff. But having lots of expensive tools isn't always necessary for building an effective engine. You can rent and borrow tools for the jobs you are only going to do once. Everything else, such as a socket set, screwdrivers, wrenches, etc., becomes useful to other car-building efforts. These are the tools you purchase.

We suggest Sears Craftsman tools because they have a lifetime warranty, great reputation, and it seems like there's a Sears store around every corner. The Craftsman warranty is a no-nonsense, no-fine-print warranty. Bust a socket and Sears will replace it with no questions asked. Strip out a ratchet and Sears will hand you a new one or rebuild your

Engine hoists used to be a major investment. These days, you can pick one up at Sam's Club, Costco, or Harbor Freight for $200 to $250. If you're not in the mood to have a hoist just sitting around, you can rent one locally. Rent it once to pull the engine. Then, rent it again to reinstall the engine.

old one. This makes Sears Craftsman tools the best tool value there is. They're costly going in, but worth every penny when it's time to get to work. The next best tool value going is Husky. You can find Husky tools at nearly any home improvement or hardware store for even less than Craftsman, yet with the same no-nonsense lifetime warranty.

Here's what you're going to need to get started:

- Set of Common and Phillips Head Screwdrivers of all sizes.
- Set of open-/box- end wrenches (1/4", 5/16", 11/32", 3/8", 7/16", 1/2", 9/16", 5/8", 11/16", 3/4", 7/8", 15/16", and 1")
- 3/8" Drive Socket Set (3/8", 7/16", 1/2", 9/16", 5/8", 11/16", and 3/4")
- 3/8" Deep Well Sockets (3/8", 7/16", 1/2", 9/16", 5/8", 11/16", and 3/4")
- 1/2" Drive Socket Set (7/16", 1/2", 9/16", 5/8", 11/16", 3/4", 7/8", 15/16", 1", 1-1/16", 1-1/8", and 1-1/4")
- 1/2" Drive Deep Well Sockets (7/16", 1/2", 9/16", 5/8", 11/16", 3/4", 7/8", 15/16", 1", 1-1/16", 1-1/8", and 1-1/4")
- 1/2" Drive Breaker Bar
- Pliers
- Needle Nose Pliers

The list of tools you could buy for engine work is virtually endless. We suggest a high-quality 1/4-, 3/8-, and 1/2-inch drive socket set. You need shallow and deep-well sockets, and it's a good idea to have a breaker bar in each set. Extensions of various lengths are important. You can really take it to the limit with both 6- and 12-point sockets for a wide variety of applications. And one more thing – if you work on late-model domestic and import vehicles, you're going to need both SAE and metric sizes.

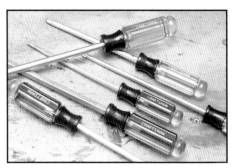

Sears Craftsman screwdrivers are an excellent investment because they will last you a lifetime with proper treatment. Opt for the largest screwdriver set Craftsman has – with every common and Phillips-head screwdriver imaginable. When you're shopping screwdrivers, shop for feel – a screwdriver that feels good to hold in your hand.

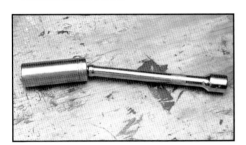

You've got to like this one – a swivel extension that allows you to get into tight places. Tools like this make the going easier.

Every good mechanic needs Allen wrenches. Get yourself a set of both SAE and metric sizes. Don't do this one on the cheap; get Allen wrenches that are high-carbon steel.

PRECISION MEASUREMENT

A degree wheel is one of those specialty tools you're not always going to need. You can rent a degree wheel and pointer locally.

Thickness gauges are something every car enthusiast should have. Go for the thickest gauges, with the greatest variety of thicknesses.

Putty knives and gasket scrapers are very necessary for tearing down an engine.

A harmonic balancer puller is necessary for engine disassembly. These can also be rented, especially if you're only going to use it once.

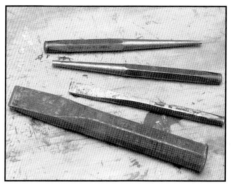

Chisels have to be purchased carefully. First, choose high-carbon tool steel for durability and safety. Don't be cheap about your chisels. They can shatter, causing injury and damage.

You can fill an entire tool drawer with holding devices – like Channel Locks, pliers, diagonal cutting pliers, duck-bill pliers, you name it. Again, spend the money and get the best tools for your investment dollar.

Specialty tools, like this long-handled ratchet from Craftsman, make the job easier because they give you a mechanical advantage. Use this type of ratchet to break a stubborn nut or bolt loose.

One of the best investments you can make is a good 1/2-inch drive torque wrench. Although you might be tempted to rent one of these, it is wise to purchase one from Sears or Harbor Freight. This is a tool you will find use for in a wide variety of applications, including your engine.

We have seen a wide variety of vice-grip types. However, there is really only one Vice-Grip brand, and their tools are worth every penny. These durable locking pliers hold just about anything you're working with.

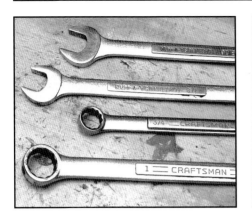

While you're buying tools, don't forget the basics: combination wrenches ranging from 1/4-inch to 1-1/8-inch.

Craftsman has this new ratcheting-style combination wrench that enables you to loosen a nut or bolt like you would with a socket wrench.

Adjustable crescent wrenches are a toolbox must. These are the new Craftsman Professional Series adjustable wrenches, available from Sears.

- Diagonal Cutting Pliers
- C-Clip Pliers
- Set of Vice Grips (Vice Grip brand only!)
- Set of Punches
- Small and Large Hammers
- A Five-Pound Sledge Hammer
- Torque Wrench (optional, but a great investment)
- Drill and Bits (spend the money and opt for high-quality bits)
- Putty Knife or Gasket Scraper
- Hack Saw (use 24 teeth-inch for best results with metal)
- Magnetic Bolt Tray
- Large Top Chest or Heavy Duty Tool Box with drawers

This list is suggested to get you started, but these tools will last you the rest of your life if you take care of them. Most of us buy socket sets, but we forget to go for the deep-well sockets, which you will need in the course of an engine build. And one other thing – opt for 6-point sockets as well as 12-point. A 6-point socket won't strip a bolt head and provides a firm grip, but the 12-point socket is easier to fit when you're working in a tight location. Make sure your socket sets have at least two extensions: one 3-inch and one 7-inch. Spring for the universal adapter as well for easy access. If you can afford it, buy a matching set of 12-point shallow and deep well sockets because they do have a purpose with some engine applications.

When you're shopping for screwdrivers, hold one in your hand first. You want a screwdriver that feels good in your hand and offers adequate grip, comfort, and mechanical advantage. If your hand slips around the handle, then it is a poor design. The tip should be super-tough tool steel that will not strip out or break. Cheap screwdrivers always strip and break. Go the extra mile and invest wisely now in a screwdriver or screwdriver set that will last you a lifetime. Another idea is to buy screwdrivers with bright orange handles for visibility and safety. This lessons the chance that you'll leave them where they don't belong.

We push the idea of quality tools because there really is a difference. Low-buck wrench sets you can buy for nine bucks won't get the job done effectively, at least not for very long. Cheap forged or cast tools will tend to strip out and leave you hanging on a Sunday afternoon when you need them most. With Craftsman, Husky, MAC, or Snap-on tools, you get a lifetime warranty you can count on. And it's a warranty that's good for as long as the tool exists – for you, your child, your grandchild, great grandchild, and more. MAC and Snap-On tools tend to be very expensive and available only off the sales truck or their company websites, which makes Craftsman and Husky a better value and easier to find.

Proper tool care is important in keeping your tools clean and serviceable. Lubricate ratchets periodically with engine oil or white grease for best

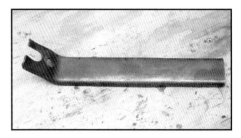

This is a valvespring compressor you can use with the cylinder heads installed on the engine. Whenever you use a compressor like this one, extra care must be taken to ensure the valve does not fall into the cylinder. Make sure the piston is at top-dead-center when you remove a valvespring.

This is a pushrod checker from Lunati Cams, which enables you to choose the right length pushrod for your small-block application. This tool also allows you to check rocker-arm geometry.

results. Drill bits should be sharpened periodically. Don't waste your money on cheap drill bits; buy only the very best. And when you're using a drill, run the bit slowly and keep it wet with

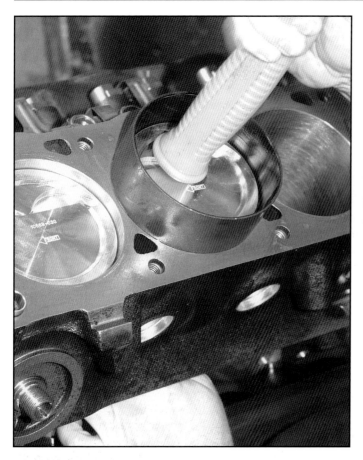

This is a brake cylinder hone, which works very well in lifter bores to improve oil control. You want the same kind of cross-hatch pattern in the lifter bores that you have in the cylinder bores.

Piston-ring compressors come in all types. This is a billet piston-ring compressor, which is the best way to go if you build a lot of engines. It's also very expensive. For the average Joe, who builds an engine every so many years, an adjustable band-type piston-ring compressor is enough – and a whole lot cheaper.

lubrication. Drill bits begin to squeak whenever they're dull. Invest in a drill-bit sharpener or find a reliable shop in town that sharpens drill bits. Just about anyone who sharpens lawnmower blades and chain saws can sharpen your drill bits.

One other thing: know when it's time to retire tools. Tools that are broken and unusable can be dangerous. A loose hammerhead, for example, could rearrange someone's dental work, break a window, or dent a fender. Cracked sockets, worn wrenches, busted screwdriver handles, and stripped ratchets mean it's time to invest in fresh equipment. Your safety and the integrity of your work are important.

A good rule of thumb when you are buying tools is to purchase them as you need them. It's a good idea to start with everything we've addressed here. However, once you have the basics in place, spend money on tools only as you need to. This frees up cash for more important things – like engine parts!

TOOLS YOU SHOULD RENT

These are the tools you're going to use only during an engine build and probably won't need again until the next engine project. These are the tools you should consider renting on an as-needed basis. Some of them might border on being tools to buy; just be realistic about how often you think you'll actually use them.

- Torque Wrench
- Piston-Ring Compressor
- Harmonic Balancer Puller
- Valvespring Compressor
- Freeze Plug Driver
- Seal Driver
- Thread Chaser
- Small Grinder (if you port your own heads)
- Easy Outs (for broken bolts in blocks and heads)
- Engine Hoist
- Engine Stand
- Degree Wheel & Pointer
- Dial Indicator

Torque wrenches typically are either beam or breakaway types. We suggest the breakaway type that clicks when you reach the specified torque. What's more, learn how to properly use a breakaway torque wrench. Two very important issues apply here: Never use a torque wrench to loosen hardware. This will throw it out of calibration. Secondly, never over torque a fastener – ever. When you torque a fastener, you are stretching the bolt stock. If you apply too much torque, you stress the fastener. Specified torque readings are there to ensure fastener integrity. Another important point about torque wrenches is calibration. Have your torque wrench cleaned, lubricated, and calibrated at least once a year for best results.

Piston-ring compressors are available in different forms. The most common type you will be able to rent is an adjustable band type. There is also a ratcheting type that makes piston installation a snap. Custom-sized billet ring compressors are costly and not for the novice. Engine-building professionals who build a lot of engines invest in billet ring compressors because getting the job done quickly is important to these folks.

A harmonic balancer puller is a borderline rental item, since you may use it again and again, and they aren't that expensive. Balancer pullers also make great steering wheel pullers. Look for the "multi-purpose" factor in any tool you're thinking about renting. If you expect to use the tool again, it may well be worth the investment now.

There are two basic types of valvespring compressors: one you use in the shop, which looks like a huge C-clamp, and one you use with the head installed (more like a pry bar). For engine rebuilding, you're going to need the C-clamp type. You can sometimes pick these up at a discount house, like Harbor Freight, for less than it would cost to rent one for a few days.

Freeze plug and seal drivers are also borderline items you could use again and again. Some people use a like-sized socket as a driver on the end of an extension. This saves money, but it could damage the socket. Don't be a tool abuser.

Thread chasers are a vital part of any engine build because you want clean threads. Clean threads yield an accurate torque reading when it's time to reassemble the engine. It's a good idea to chase every bolt hole. When a thread chaser is outside of your budget, use Grade 8 bolts and other fasteners with WD-40 to chase the threads. This may sound crude, but it will save you money and still get the job done.

Tools should be rented only at the time you intend to use them. Don't rent every tool mentioned here at the same time, because you're not going to use all of them at once. Thread chasing, for example, should be performed when the block returns from the machine shop clean, machined, and ready for assembly. Machine shops that are on the ball will have already chased your threads. Remember, thread chasing is time consuming, so some machine shops don't generally do this unless asked and paid for the service.

Engine stands are one of those purchase/rent questions because renting can sometimes cost you more than simply buying, since they can be cheap depending on where you buy. Harbor Freight has some of the best values going at $50 to $100 for a stand, but don't cut corners here. Invest in a four-legged engine stand for stability and safety. The low-buck $50 may not stand up under the weight of a heavy engine, and we don't even want to get into what it's like when an engine stand fails – it's sudden, noisy, and destructive.

The decision to rent or buy tools boils down to how often you will use the tool, and how long you will need it during your engine build. Any time you're going to need the tool longer than one to three days, you're probably better off buying. If you have to buy, look on the bright side. You can always loan it to friends or sell it after your engine is finished. Keeping it makes it a useful piece of community property among friends, and the guy with all the tools is always popular.

As long as we are on the subject of support equipment, don't forget a good engine hoist, which can also be a valuable piece of community property. When you considering renting or buying an engine hoist, buying one seems to make more economic sense these days. Did you know you can pick up a good engine hoist at Costco or Sam's for under $200? If three or four people go in on the purchase of a hoist, it becomes very affordable. These affordable hoists fold up and roll out of the way when they're not in use, and set-up time is a matter of minutes.

Another very important issue is jacks and jack stands. It's well documented that inferior jacks and jack stands do get people hurt and killed each year. Buy only the best jack stands that are made out of angle iron and welded together with solid integrity. Make sure the jack stand is more than able to support the weight of your vehicle. That doesn't mean using one jack stand to support the entire vehicle; it means going a little overboard so you know your jacks will support con-siderably more weight than they'll ever have to.

Absolutely never lay under a vehicle supported by a hydraulic jack or mechanical bumper jack. These jacks are not fail safe. They can fail with unspeakable consequences. Jack stands, properly positioned beneath frame rails on a level surface, offer the best protection. Make sure your jack and jack stands are always in good, serviceable condition. Keep hydraulic jacks in the "down" position whenever they aren't in use. This keeps dust and moisture off the ram. If you allow the ram to get rusty, the rust will cut the seals, rendering the jack useless. Also exercise this practice with an engine hoist by keeping the arm in the "down" position whenever the hoist isn't in use.

KEEP A CLEAN WORK SHOP

We cannot stress enough the importance of keeping a clean, organized shop. Do your engine teardown work where you can catalog everything and keep parts in their rightful places. Keep engine parts and fasteners in jars or plastic containers that are labeled with a marker. Haul the block, heads, crankshaft, and connecting rods to a machine shop immediately upon disassembly. This avoids any confusion and keeps you moving on your engine build.

If you cannot afford the machine work and all the parts at once, leave the engine assembled until you can afford it. We speak from experience on this one: too much is lost both mentally and physically once the engine is disassembled. Keep disassembly, cleaning, machine work, and assembly as close together as possible.

It's a good idea to know what you're going to do and when you're going to do it in the course of an engine build. This book will help you form your plan. Then get busy and see your engine project through to completion. Nothing is more discouraging than a disassembled engine that's going nowhere because you didn't have a plan.

Building a Stroker

An engine's stroke is determined by taking the distance from the crankshaft centerline to the center of the journal and multiplying it by 2. If we have 1-1/2 inches between the crankshaft and rod journal centerlines, we have 3 inches of stroke.

The greater the distance between the crankshaft and rod journal centerlines, the greater the stroke. To increase stroke, we increase this distance. This is done using a crankshaft with a greater throw, or welding and offset grinding the rod journal on an existing crankshaft. You can achieve significant stroke increases by offset grinding an existing crankshaft.

If we opt for a custom crankshaft with even greater stroke, we can achieve a 3.50-inch stroke, which balloons our 302 into a 355.

Rod length matters just as much as stroke. A longer connecting rod allows the piston to dwell longer at the bottom and top of the cylinder bore, which allows for a greater fuel/air charge.

This is the kind of piston design you want to avoid if reliability and long engine life are your goal. Keep the piston pin out of the ring area. Having the piston pin close to the hot piston crown is asking for premature engine failure because oil struggles to stay on the pin and boss. Heat chases the oil away.

ENGINE DISASSEMBLY

One of the most fascinating parts of an engine rebuild is the teardown. During an engine teardown, you can learn a great deal about how the engine ran, how it was treated, and how its many components wore in during its service life. Hammered rod bearings indicate hard use and abuse. Scuffed cylinder walls indicate oil starvation issues and high operating temperatures. Valves worn deep into the seats indicate a poorly executed valve job or hard use with unleaded fuels.

The area you should be concerned with most is the cylinder block and its many dimensions. Ideally, you will find a block with standard 4.000-inch bores that has never been rebuilt. A 289/302/351W block that has been

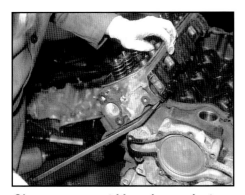

Gloves are a great idea when you're tearing down your engine – it will be dirty. Take your time, and be careful not to drop anything on your foot.

bored .020- or .030-inch oversize can go one more oversize up to 4.040 inches, but that's it. The 351C can go as high as 4.060-inches, but no more.

Although quite a few builders push the 289/302/351W to 4.060-inches, this is strongly discouraged because the lightweight gray-wall iron cylinder walls are quite thin. Taking bore size to 4.060 inches is courting trouble, but doing it without sonic-checking the block is foolish. By taking the bore size to 4.060 inches, you drive the compression ratio higher, which raises operating temperatures and pressures. With a larger bore, we drive compression higher by increasing the volume we squeeze into the existing combustion chamber. Because cylinder wall thickness is marginal at best at this oversize, you also risk getting into the water jackets. So, take it from us – do not go above 4.040-inches on bore size with any small-block Ford.

THE TEARDOWN

In Chapter 1, we told you about our subject engine, a 1965 289-2V engine removed from Jeff Fischbach's Mustang convertible. When *Mustang Monthly* decided to target this engine for a "Budget 289 Build-Up" last year, they invited us to follow to gather information for this book. The engine had failed coming off of a Los Angeles freeway. Suddenly, it

had no power and developed a horrible knock in rhythm with the crankshaft. When *Mustang Monthly* Senior Editor Jim Smart was troubleshooting the noise, he knew it was serious. He started by shorting each of the spark plugs out one at a time. When he pulled the number-4 spark plug wire, the knock stopped – a bad sign. He also did a compression check. All cylinders checked healthy except for number 4 – which came in low. Pouring some oil into number-4 cylinder and checking compression showed a big improvement – another bad sign. Cylinder sealing on number-4 was poor for a reason. The piston was cracked, which allowed compression to escape. That cracking also caused the knock.

Jim also learned in the course of the teardown that number-5 cylinder on the opposite bank was in all kinds of trouble, too, even though compression checked within limits. Coolant was leaking into cylinder number 5 from a defective head gasket while the engine sat. Compression from the number-5 cylinder undoubtedly leaked into the water jacket, aggravating overheating issues already caused by the right-bank cylinder-head gasket being installed backwards during the last rebuild.

What we learned from this teardown is something we hope you'll learn from this book – what not to do when you rebuild your small-block Ford. Because our 289 engine experienced a

This is our rebuild candidate for this book – a 1965 289-2V engine from a Mustang convertible. It has experienced at least one rebuild by a Los Angeles area mass-production rebuilder. The prognosis for this engine isn't good. It appears well maintained and clean inside, thanks to regular oil and filter changes, but improper assembly by the rebuilder caused it to fail.

really sloppy mass-production-style rebuild at some time in its past, it was not properly machined and assembled, which led to the failure. We're going to talk about this failure in great detail to help you avoid the same mistakes. We're also going to address common mistakes that cause a lot of engine failures.

Jeff's 289 engine failed for two fundamental reasons – the water pump wasn't installed properly (no backing plate), and the right-bank cylinder-head gasket was installed backwards. The backward cylinder-head gasket is an easy mistake to make because it isn't very apparent at first glance. It happens whenever we're not paying attention to what we're doing during an engine build. Each and every head gasket has "FRONT" stamped in the surface to ensure proper installation, but people mix it up all the time building Ford V-8s. Cooling passages in the cylinder-head gasket must always go at the rear of the block to ensure proper cool-

ing. This allows coolant to circulate completely through the block and heads on its way to the thermostat and radiator.

Whenever we install both head gaskets backwards, trouble begins the minute we fire a new engine. If we get both head gaskets backwards, overheating will become apparent immediately. Whenever you install a small-block Ford cylinder-head gasket backwards, coolant flow is cut off to the rear of the block and cylinder heads. Coolant then circulates only at the front of the block and heads, causing a large percentage of the engine to overheat. In this case, only the right bank ran hot because a significant percentage of the coolant was allowed to circulate and cool normally.

In time, engine oil broke down on the extremely hot surfaces – cylinder walls, pistons and rings, bearings, valveguides, and more. Because cylinder number 4 suffered the greatest amount of thermal abuse, it failed first. Extreme heat cracked the piston from the crown to the skirt. It probably wasn't noticeable until the piston cracked all the way through, when a horrible misfire and knock developed.

Jeff's engine failure wasn't something that happened overnight. It happened over a period of many years. Heat went to work on the rear of the right bank of cylinders, resulting in eventual failure. Had he continued to drive the car the way it was, the engine would have seized due to total number-4 piston failure. Had that not done him in, cylinder number 5 on the left bank would have finished the engine off by drawing coolant into the cylinder bore.

Let's take this idea a step further. Had the car sat for several months, coolant would have filled cylinder number 5, causing a nasty hydro-lock the first time Jeff tried to start the

engine. Hydro-lock is what happens when we try compressing fluid in the area above the piston. Because fluid cannot be compressed, more fragile elements (piston, rod, and block) are compromised instead. Typically, the piston and rod both fail – even causing the cylinder wall to crumble in the process. We have seen hydro-locked engines in which the cylinder wall failed right along with the piston and rod, causing coolant to flood the oil pan. In this case the hydro-lock would have bent or snapped the number-5 connecting rod, and even could have broken the crankshaft.

Jeff probably noticed his Mustang's temperature gauge running on the high side, especially during hot weather, but it was never quite hot enough to boil over. As Jeff, and earlier his uncle, drove the Mustang, the right bank of cylinders ran very hot without notice. Adding insult to injury was the fact that the water pump was installed without a backing plate, which further aggravated cooling issues. Without the steel backing plate, coolant was never properly channeled through the pump and the water jackets, making a hot-spot situation even worse. In this case, the water pump impeller contacted the timing cover due to the missing plate. Why anyone removed this plate in the first place is beyond us. In any case, it all contributed to engine failure.

Since the owner, Jeff Fischbach, wants this engine to be kept original, he has elected to go with a factory cast-iron four-barrel intake manifold with the correct Autolite 4100 carburetor. We can improve its performance without adversely affecting originality.

1 Remove and Inspect the Flywheel

1–Jim Grubbs Motorsports is going to rebuild our 289 engine. Disassembly is organized, with all parts being cataloged and properly stored. Knowing which parts came from where helps us to determine why this engine failed. First, we remove the flywheel, which needs resurfacing. The flywheel suffers from heat cracking because the clutch disc was improperly installed.

2 Remove the Separator Plate

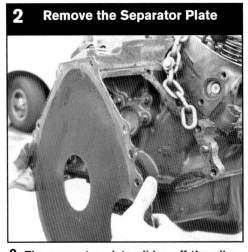

2–The separator plate slides off the alignment dowels on the back of the block.

SPECIAL TOOL USED

3 Put the Engine on an Engine Stand

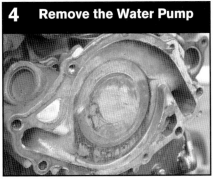

3–Once the separator plate and flywheel are removed, the engine is fitted to an engine stand for the teardown. You can buy an affordable engine stand from Harbor Freight for around $75. We suggest one with four casters for the best stability. Notice the rebuilder's overheated detector at the freeze plug on the right-hand cylinder head. It indicates an overheat (the dot) – actually the rebuilder's fault in this case.

4 Remove the Water Pump

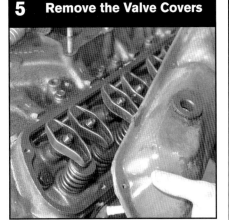

4–Engine failure happens for all kinds of reasons. Here's one. When the water pump was replaced, someone forgot to use the steel cover that goes on the back of the water pump. That's why the impeller ground this circle into the timing cover. Not only is impeller contact with the timing cover unacceptable, but coolant flow was also hindered by the absence of the plate. This is one reason why this engine ran so hot.

5 Remove the Valve Covers

5–Both valve covers are removed. This engine, for all the heat damage we found, was surprisingly clean inside.

6 Remove the Intake Manifold

6–The intake manifold bolts are removed next. Place these bolts in a plastic container and label it so you can find the bolts when you need them. Remove the intake manifold.

7   Remove the Rocking Arms

7–Next, remove all rocker arms as shown. Keep them lined up with the cylinders they came off of. This enables you to examine wear patterns. Here's one result of sloppy mass-production rebuilding – incorrect valves. On one bank, we have the correct valvestem length, short and flush with the top of the retainer. On the other bank, we have longer valvestems, designed for mid-1966 to '77 small-blocks with rail-style rocker arms. Note the longer valvestem tip, designed for the rail-style rocker arm. This throws the rocker-arm geometry off with 1962 to early 1966-style rocker arms.

8   Remove the Cylinder Heads

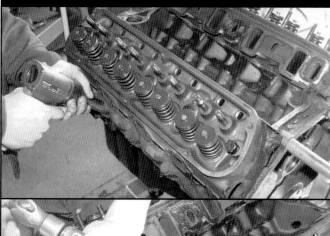

8–Remove all of the cylinder head bolts and put them in a labeled plastic container. Take your time. You need an organized teardown, with all fasteners properly cataloged for proper assembly later on. Cylinder heads are pried from the block. Hold onto the cylinder heads when you are prying them loose. They can slide off the block dowels and land on your feet. Take extra care when you are removing the heads, and keep track of which bank each head came from.

9   Inspect the Head Gaskets

9–This 289 sat for a year after it failed. Look what coolant leaking into cylinder number 5 from a defective head gasket did. Electrolysis between the aluminum piston and iron cylinder, via the coolant, caused the piston to corrode badly. Coolant came from this water jacket into the bore.

PRECISION MEASUREMENT
10   Measure the Bores

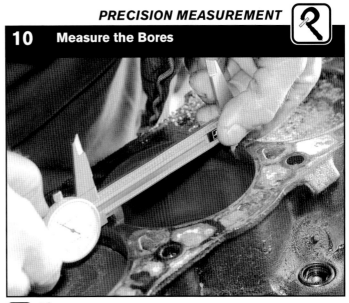

10–Measuring the cylinder bore with a micrometer (called "miking" the bore) brings bad news. Jeff's block has already been bored .040-inch oversize. We could bore it to .060-inch oversize, but this would be a risky practice. We need a replacement block.

11   Inspect the Bores

11–Our 289 engine didn't live very long after its previous rebuild. There are no ridges at the tops of the cylinder bores, which happens as piston rings wear into the cylinder walls short of the top of the cylinder. These are cheap cast .040-inch oversize pistons.

12   Disassemble the Intake for Cleaning

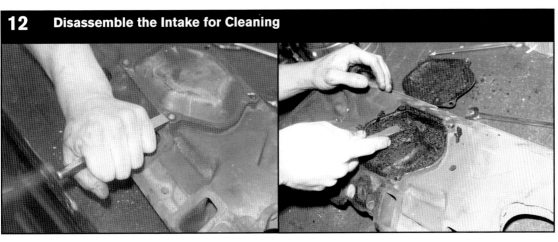

12–The C5AE four-barrel intake manifold is disassembled for cleaning. The manifold heat stove cover is removed as shown. Then, the manifold goes into a cleaning machine, which tumbles the iron with steel shot for a "like-new" appearance.

13   Clean the Intake

13–This is the cleaning machine composed of a rolling carrier that exposes the iron pieces to steel shot, which is blasted against the iron. When these parts come out, they will look like brand new iron.

IMPORTANT STEP **!**

14   Inspect the Harmonic Balancer

! *14–The harmonic balancer is 40 years old and needs to be replaced because the rubber has deteriorated. We will toss this one and replace it with a new one.*

15   Remove the Harmonic Balancer

15–The harmonic balancer is removed next using a puller. Remove the large crankshaft bolt first. Then, screw the bolt back in a couple of threads for the puller to have something to work against.

16   Removing Timing Cover and Set

16–Remove the timing cover and timing set. Examine the chain for stretching. Excessive stretch tells us something about wear patterns in the chain, gears, and block.

17   Remove the Oil Pump

17–After you have removed the oil pan, remove the oil pump and shaft. We suggest replacing the shaft and pump. An oil pan with a stripped-out drain plug should be replaced.

18 Remove the Rods and Pistons

18–Piston and connecting rod removal is next. Remove the rod bolt nuts and gently tap the rod bolts as shown with a hammer, pushing the piston and rod out through the top of the block. As with the rocker arms mentioned earlier, keep the pistons and rods with the cylinders they came out of for wear-inspection purposes.

19 Inspect the Rod Bearings

19–Close inspection of this rod bearing reveals some bad news. Look at the damage to this rod bearing from excessive engine heat and oil breakdown. With oil breakdown came excessive friction, grinding the bearing down to the copper.

20 Remove and Inspect the Main Caps

20–The main bearing caps are removed next. Like the rod bearings, close inspection of the main bearings tells a story about poor engine assembly technique. Look at this badly scored main bearing. A piece of dirt got in there during assembly. When the engine was started, the grain of dirt was ground into the bearing. A close study of the main bearing journals shows excessive heat damage. Oil breakdown here caused excessive scoring.

21   Remove the Crankshaft

21–The crankshaft is removed next. Remember what your mother (and OSHA) always told you: Lift with your legs – not your back – to prevent back injury.

24   Remove the Rear Main Seal

24–The rear main seal is removed and tossed. Wear issues are important here, too. Inspect the number-5 main journal and seal lip while you're here. This, of course, does not apply to late-model 5.0L engines with one-piece rear main seals. It does, however, apply inspection-wise. Always check the seal contact areas. Scored seal contact surfaces mean oil leakage later on.

22   Inspect the Crankshaft

22–The crankshaft journals are measured with a micrometer. These journals have already been machined down .020 inch and are badly scored. We could machine this crankshaft to .030-inch undersize. Instead, we're going to find another "1M" crankshaft.

23   Inspect the Main Bearing

23–Remove all of the main bearings, inspect the wear patterns, and throw them away. We inspect wear patterns because we want to know the history of the crankshaft. If the crank is distorted or bent, main bearings will be excessively worn toward the sides and radiuses.

25   Remove the Camshaft and Lifters

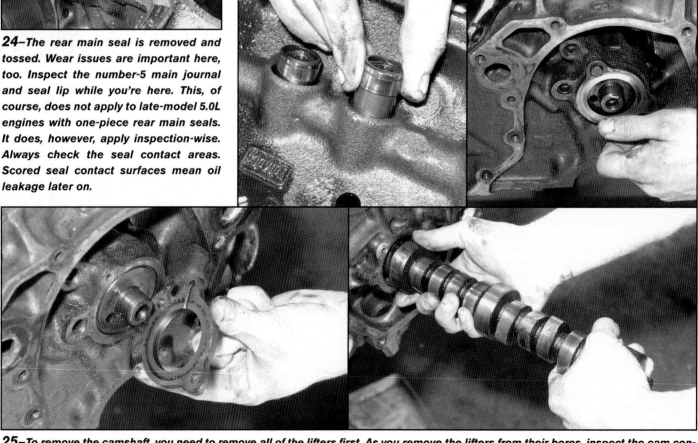

25–To remove the camshaft, you need to remove all of the lifters first. As you remove the lifters from their bores, inspect the cam contact surfaces for wear patterns. Once the lifters are removed, remove the front cam retainer plate by removing the two bolts. Then, gently slip the cam out of the block.

26 Inspect the Lifters

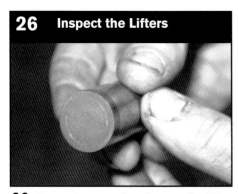

26–Excessive and abnormal lifter wear tells us this engine suffered from oil breakdown, which happens with overheating.

IMPORTANT STEP !

27 Remove Freeze Plugs

! *27–Remove all of the freeze plugs and oil galley plugs. This enables the machine shop to clean out the water jackets and oil galleys. The block needs to be completely bare.*

28 Remove the Cam Bearings

28–Cam bearings are removed next using a cam bearing installation tool. Bearings are removed from the front of the block, working toward the back. We knock them out the same way we install them. These cam bearings were badly damaged during installation. Oil breakdown from extreme heat also did a lot of damage.

29 Remove the Oil Galley Plug

29–There is an oil galley plug at the top of the block, located beneath the intake manifold. Remove this plug, which makes way for a more thorough block cleaning.

IMPORTANT STEP **!**

30 Remove the Cam Plug

! *30–The screw-in oil galley plugs at the rear of the block must be removed. Don't forget to remove the cam plug.*

31

31–Remove the screw-in oil filter adaptor.

32 Inspect the Chambers

32–Inspection of the right cylinder head shows evidence of a troubled number-4 cylinder (bottom chamber). Notice how dark the chamber is from a lack of compression and oil burning. The rest are normal, with white exhaust valves and tan chambers.

33 Remove the Valves

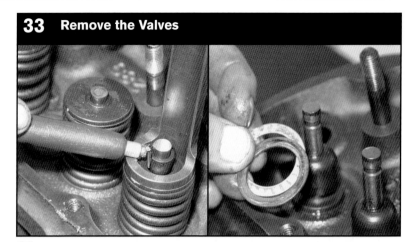

33–Cylinder head disassembly begins one valve at a time. Each spring is compressed and the two keepers are removed. Sometimes, valvespring retainers and keepers become seized. It's a good idea to whack on the side of the retainer with a hammer, and then compress the spring again when the keepers stick. All eight valves from each head need to be lined up for inspection to determine wear patterns that need your attention.

34 Inspect the Valves

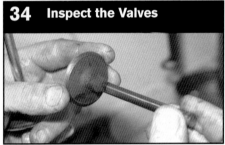

34–Each valve is inspected closely. This cylinder head has obviously been apart before and had a valve job. The valve faces show abnormal wear to the point that they were sinking deeply into the seats.

35 Inspect the Valve Seats

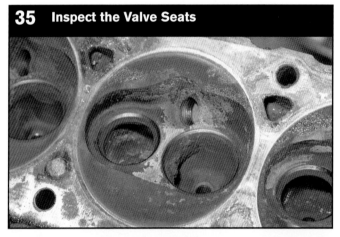

35–When we look at the valve seats, the valve face's condition makes sense. A bad valve job (improper seat and valve face angle) has caused the valves to wear deeply into the seats. All 16 valves and seats will have to be replaced.

36 Inspect the Valveguides

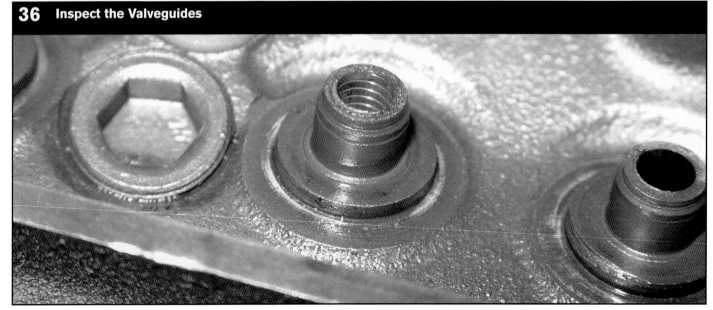

36–Our cylinder heads send a mixed message. Some valveguides are bronze – some are not. We are replacing all 16 guides for uniformity.

WHY DO ENGINES WEAR OUT?

Automobile engines have a tough job to do. For the most part, they do it well for many years and thousands of miles reliably. Trouble abounds when we don't take care of them, or when we put them together improperly. When we do take good care of them, engines can last between 100,000 and 200,000 miles. Depending on how much you drive, that's about five to ten years of use. With a new timing set and oil pump at 120,000 to 150,000 miles, along with regular oil and filter service every 3,000 to 5,000 miles, you might see in excess of 250,000 miles from your engine.

The greatest rider you can put on your engine's life insurance policy is regularly-scheduled oil and filter changes using Mobil 1 synthetic engine oil and a Wix or Motorcraft oil filter. With clean oil in the pan, you're assured a solid barrier between all moving parts inside your small-block. And when you use synthetic engine oil, it stays on moving parts, even when an engine sits for days. This affords you good protection during start-up.

Another important point is regular cooling-system service. The wise enthusiast will flush and service the cooling system every spring or fall. If it's hard to remember to do that, opt for cooling-system service every two years. You can get away with some degree of cooling-system neglect when you're running iron cylinder heads. Whenever you step up to aluminum heads, you are mixing dissimilar metals that don't like each other. Aluminum particles wind up attached to iron castings – and vice versa. The result is corrosion. This is one reason why we don't see copper and brass radiators in new cars anymore. Other reasons include weight and cost; aluminum radiators with plastic tanks are lighter and cheaper.

So why do engines wear out? Engines wear out mostly due to dirty oil, poor filtration, poor tuning, neglect, and even improper assembly to begin with. If an engine is built with poor dynamic balancing, vibration will shorten its life. If main and rod bearing side clearances are too tight, expect a short trip. Piston-to-cylinder-wall clearances are yet another reason. This is why checking and rechecking clearances during the build up is so important.

Valvetrain issues are likely the greatest cause of engine failure. This encompasses a lot of items – burned valves, worn stems and guides, excessive rocker-arm wear, wiped cam lobes, worn lifters, and timing chain and gear failure. The greatest area of neglect we see time and time again is the timing set. When our small-block Fords were young, most of them had nylon-coated aluminum timing gears. Ford did this to help make the timing set run quieter. We have replaced an untold numbers of nylon and aluminum gears with steel gears over the past 40 years. I've never been able to hear the difference in the steel gear or chain.

Many people tend to whistle in the dark when it comes to timing sets. They're like that elephant in the living room that no one wants to talk about. Timing sets are a pain in the neck to replace, which is why we continue to put replacement off. And then they fail, often with catastrophic results. With the nylon-coated aluminum cam gears, both aluminum and nylon crumble and flow into the oil pan. When they do, they wind up in the oil pump and bearings. Finally, main, rod, and cam bearings are damaged from the debris.

Sometimes, timing sets are replaced with no regard for the debris that got into the oil pan. We press them back into service, with serious fluctuations in oil pressure and volume. If we're lucky, we'll get an "oil" or "check engine" light and have sense enough to pull the oil pan and clean out the debris. Some people will just push the engine until it fails.

Engines also fail from poor tuning technique – too much timing or too little. Too much timing hurts the engine by changing the way the air/fuel mix ignites in the chamber. The more we advance the timing, the longer the flame travel and the higher the combustion temperatures. With this advance in ignition timing, we create hot spots – additional ignition sources that create colliding flame fronts and shock waves across the top of the piston. This is known as detonation, or the "pinging" we hear in spark knock under hard acceleration.

Advancing the timing in healthy increments helps us make power. However, too much timing (too much advance) can do permanent engine damage. Late ignition timing won't hurt the engine as badly as too much advance. However, late ignition timing sends high combustion temperatures teaming toward exhaust stroke. This causes exhaust valves and headers to run considerably hotter. It also robs us of power.

An extremely lean fuel mixture that comes from improper carburetor jetting or a worn-out fuel pump can cause serious engine damage. If your engine has electronic fuel injection, faulty sensors will create all kinds of grief. Faulty oxygen sensors can cause extremes in fuel mixture – either overly rich or extremely lean. Coolant temperature, manifold air pressure, throttle position, inlet air temperature, and mass-air sensors can become defective, adversely affecting fuel mixture and spark curves.

There are engine failure issues that aren't as obvious as some of the items we've covered here. The use of incorrect parts is one of them. Our 289 had two different valvestem lengths, which adversely affected rocker-arm geometry on the left bank. This could have caused rocker-arm failure due to stress. A failing rocker arm can cause a pushrod to come right through the valve cover. It can also cause valvespring retainer failure, which causes a valve to drop into the cylinder.

Using incorrect valvesprings can cause engine failure or abnormal wear issues. Valvesprings that are too stiff can wear cam lobes and cause excessive valvestem wear. Valvesprings that are too soft can cause valve float at high revs, which can lead to engine failure. Valve float refers to runaway valves that don't seat at high revs because the valve springs aren't stiff enough to snap them closed. When valves float (stay open) at high revs, we run the risk of valve-to-piston contact, which virtually guarantees us total engine destruction. This is certainly more possible if we're running a high-lift camshaft where valve-to-piston clearances aren't much to begin with.

Using a double-roller timing chain without considering the clearance between your oil slinger, timing chain, and timing cover can cause metal trash to enter the oil, eating the main, rod, and cam bearings alive. Metal gets into the oil when the oil slinger lip rubs against the dual-roller timing chain. You can flatten the oil slinger gently with a hammer, which moves the lip away from the chain. This is best performed by using a block of wood between the hammer and oil slinger.

An oil pump driveshaft with worn ends can slip, twist, and fail, rendering the oil pump useless. When the oil pump brakes down, the engine brakes down – unless you're quick with the ignition switch.

Using rail-style rocker arms on a 1962 through early 1966 small-block Ford is a mistake we see from time to time by technicians who are not familiar with these engines. The side rails press on the valvespring retainers, especially if you use a high-lift camshaft. The repeated pressure on the retainer leads to keeper failure – and catastrophic engine damage when stray valves fall into cylinders.

Understanding Engine Failure

WORKBENCH TIP

Whenever we disassemble an engine, we have to learn to be forensics experts, able to determine what happened to our engines before they were torn down. Sometimes we rebuild engines because we want something fresh and new. And sometimes we rebuild them because they stop dead in their tracks, like Jeff's 289. In either case, we need to know what to look for during a teardown.

Before you begin a teardown, take a look at the intake and exhaust ports. Gray and tan exhaust ports are normal. White exhaust ports can mean trouble – high combustion temperatures and lean conditions. Are the exhaust ports wet or dry? Oily exhaust ports indicate faulty valveguides and seals, or piston oil-ring issues.

What about spark plugs? Spark plugs are the greatest barometer of an engine's health. White and tan spark plug insulators are normal. A spark plug with small particles on the firing tip indicates lean conditions and serious detonation. Those particles are typically bits of molten aluminum from a failing piston.

Have you ever checked your intake manifold vacuum at idle? Did you ever run a compression check with the engine warm? What was the oil pressure at a hot idle and at cruise power? Normal oil pressure should be 10 psi for every 1,000 rpm. That means you should have roughly 30 to 40 psi at cruise.

Each of these dynamics tells us about our engine's state of health without turning a bolt.

Intake manifold vacuum tells us a lot about the engine's respiratory health – cylinder and valve sealing, cam profile, intake manifold sealing, and more. We want the highest manifold vacuum possible at idle – around 18 to 22 inches. When manifold vacuum reads only 10 to 12 inches, we either have a radical camshaft or an ailing engine. Watching needle behavior on the vacuum gauge can be interesting because it, alone, tells us a lot about engine health. A bouncing needle indicates valve-seating issues. It can also indicate a wiped cam lobe.

A compression check tells us as much about an engine's health as intake manifold vacuum. Take a piece of paper and a pencil, write down cylinders 1 through 8, and check compression. The engine should be warm because cylinders won't seal as well with the engine cold. As the engine warms, pistons and rings grow in the bores, which improves cylinder sealing. The same can be said for cylinder head gaskets and the like. With heat, everything grows into right size – if it's sized properly to begin with. At operating temperature, your engine should be as healthy as it's ever going to be.

When you screw the compression gauge into each spark plug hole, make sure it's snug. It's a good idea to put engine oil on the threads and O-ring, which makes it easier to thread and improves sealing. Disconnect the ignition coil lead and have someone hold the throttle wide open. Crank the engine several revolutions until the needle has gone as far as it's going to go. When you have checked compression on all eight cylinders, how does it look across the board? Typical cranking compression pressure for a small-block Ford should be around 150 to 180 psi. If compression on all eight cylinders averages 130 psi, for example, that's still a good sign. It means compression is uniform across the board.

If one or two cylinders come in way below the others, there is a problem that needs attention. Two side-by-side bores with compression considerably lower than the rest can be blamed on a blown cylinder head gasket between those two cylinders. Worst-case scenario is a cracked cylinder head casting or block deck warpage.

Whenever a cylinder comes in at zero compression, it indicates a blown piston, failed valve, or thrown connecting rod. Even burned or cracked valves will yield some compression. The total absence of compression is serious. If a compression check shows little or no compression on all eight cylinders, it means a failed timing set or broken crankshaft. Game over...

Understanding Engine Failure (continued)

Close inspection of number-4 cylinder prior to disassembly shows us what happened. Excessive right bank heat caused the number-4 piston to crack under the stress, which also injured the cylinder wall beyond repair.

Number-4 piston cracked along its entire length from excessive heat. This caused our knock and misfire.

Not only did piston number 4 suffer damage from overheating, oil breakdown at the bearing took it right down to the copper. Look at this damage.

With the piston removed, the damage to cylinder number 4 is more apparent. Because this bore is already at 4.040 inches, this block is finished.

SELECTING PARTS

Choosing the right engine castings and parts for your application isn't as simple as it is for Chevy enthusiasts, and that's a compliment for Chevrolet in many respects. Chevrolet engine castings haven't changed much over the half-century production life of the world's most popular V-8 engine. We can't say the same thing about the small-block Ford. Ford's peppy small-block has been through untold changes since it was introduced in 1962 as the 90-degree Fairlane V-8. Although Ford buffs love to curse Father Ford, running changes are commonplace at Ford because Dearborn never remains very content with things as they are. As a result, the small-block Ford has been ever changing for more than 40 years.

Though there have been many changes in the small-block Ford over the years, the changes are simple to understand. In its original form, the 221/260/289-ci small-block had a five-bolt (narrow pattern) bellhousing pattern. We find this pattern from 1962 to '64 only. From 1965 and up, there is a six-bolt bellhousing pattern, which is the most common. This means a late-model 5.0L engine will bolt right up to a 1965 and up C4, T-10, or Top Loader transmission (wide pattern) bellhousing. It also means a 1965 and up 289/302-ci small-block will bolt right up to a late-model Automatic Overdrive or T-5 5-speed. Engine mount attachment points have never changed, which makes these swaps simple in scope.

John DaLuz of JMC Motorsports in San Diego, California, understands the importance of selecting the right parts for an engine build. John's first question for a customer is "how do you intend to drive the car?" Before you order parts, you must know how you intend to use the engine.

This is the large six-bolt bellhousing bolt pattern from 1965 to present. As you might imagine, this is a more common and logical replacement for that 1962 to 64 five-bolt block if you're not concerned about originality. With this six-bolt pattern, you open yourself up to a wider variety of transmissions and bellhousings.

This is the late-model, 5.0L roller-tappet block, an excellent foundation for any small-block Ford project. It has provisions for the roller tappets, a one-piece rear-main seal, and is designed for the serpentine belt drive in front.

Here's what you can do with a small-block Ford. Look at these five main bearings with studs. This makes the foundation nice and rigid – good for high-revving bottom ends.

Ford went from the five-bolt to the six-bolt bellhousing pattern in 1965 for one simple reason: By expanding the pattern and adding the sixth bolt, vibration and noise are distributed over a broader area, which reduced noise, vibration, and harshness. Ford did the same thing with the 170- and 200-ci sixes to quiet things down. If you're trying to improve your vintage Ford without concern for originality, ditch the five-bolt block and related transmission, and opt for a six-bolt duo. This will make things easier on you because the parts are much more common

BLOCKS

The 221- and 260-ci blocks differed from the 289/302 blocks in bore size. Neither block had a 4-inch bore, but instead they had 3.50- and 3.80-inch bores, respectively. They also employ 7/16-inch bellhousing bolts instead of 1/2-inch like we find in the 289/302 blocks. The 289 was the first small-block Ford to have a 4.000-inch bore. And

because the 302 also has a 4.000-inch bore, it has basically the same block as the 289. When Ford first began casting 302 blocks in mid 1967 (as 1968 castings), they had slightly longer cylinder skirts to give the piston greater stability at the bottom of the bore. We have documented 302 blocks in 1967 Fords with 289 internals. This proves that the Ford factory built 1967-vintage 289s using 302 blocks. We are convinced this practice continued through 1968.

Although a lot of different six-bolt block casting numbers have appeared

John Da Luz of JMC Motorsports lays in a 331-ci stroker crank, which fits nicely in the modified 5.0L block. With a little bit of work on the cylinder skirts, you can fit a 355-ci stroker crank into this block. The good news is that these new blocks are cheap.

This is the 351W block, which is based on the 289/302 block. Where this block differs is its taller deck (1.274 inches taller), which allows for a 1/2-inch longer stroke. This deck height difference makes the 351W wider than the 289/302.

The 351W block has thicker, heavier webbing than the 289/302 block.

Here is the 351C block, which doesn't really look like a small-block Ford at all. It looks more like Oldsmobile V-8 blocks of the era, with the timing set wrapped in iron, with a steel timing cover, and a fuel-pump with bolts at 12 and 6 o'clock. The 351C, and the 351/400M, were short-lived "middle-block" Ford engines produced from 1970 to 1978. Although this has been a great performance engine through the years, there are not enough rebuildable cores out there. Unless you absolutely have to have a Cleveland, we suggest going with the more plentiful 351W.

If you decide to go with a stroker kit, all you have to do is notch the cylinder skirts to clear the connecting rod bolts. This means you can pump a lot of displacement into the 5.0L (302-ci) block.

since 1965, not much has changed through the years. From 1965-84, 289/302 blocks were virtually the same except for the cast-in front accessory drive mount on the right-hand side, which first appeared with the introduction of serpentine belt drive. Another significant change was the one-piece rear main seal, which first appeared for 1985. Crankshafts are not interchangeable at this point. Crankshafts with the lip for a two-piece seal will not work in the one-piece seal block. By the same token, the lipless one-piece seal crank will not work in a two-piece seal block because it will leak. The lip works hand in hand with the two-piece seal. Without the lip, it's a leaker.

Two types of small-block castings had wider main bearing caps – the 289 High Performance block and all Mexican-block 289s and 302s. Contrary to what we have all been told through the years, it turns out Mexican blocks are not made of high-nickel iron. They weigh virtually the same as their U.S. counterparts. The only benefit is the wider main caps we find south of the border.

221/260/289/302 CYLINDER HEADS

Outside of the five-to-six-bolt bellhousing pattern change for 1965, the next most significant change for

the small-block Ford is valvetrain and valve covers in 1966. On May 8, 1966, Ford went to a rail-style rocker arm on the small-block Ford. Instead of a pushrod guide hole cast into the cylinder head, the rail-style rocker arm sat on a taller valvestem, which kept the rocker centered on the valve. At first thought, this is a good idea. But, when you consider engine wear and the possibility of using a high-performance camshaft, this idea is a bad one. As the valvestem tip wears, the side rails get closer and closer to the retainer. Eventually, they work their way into the retainer, which can fail, drop the valve, and destroy the engine. Throw in a high-performance, high-lift camshaft, and engine failure becomes probable.

Ford Casting Identification

WORKBENCH TIP

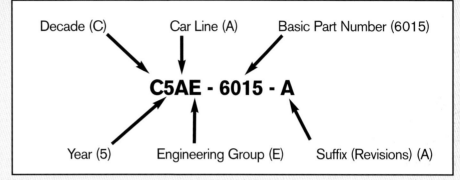

Decade (C) — Car Line (A) — Basic Part Number (6015)

C5AE - 6015 - A

Year (5) — Engineering Group (E) — Suffix (Revisions) (A)

Ford made it easy to identify castings and forgings via its casting numbers and date codes. This makes it possible to identify the year, engineering changes, and the exact date something was made. Here's how it works.

TYPICAL FORD PART/CASTING NUMBER

It's easy to identify Ford castings once you understand the system because there's not only a casting number, but a casting date code that tells you exactly when the piece was cast. There's also a date code stamped in the piece that tells us the date of manufacture. With these two date codes, we know when the piece was cast and when it was ultimately manufactured.

Ford part numbers can be found in the Ford Master Parts Catalog on microfilm at your Ford dealer or in one of those obsolete 900-pound parts catalogs from the good old days. Because Ford has obsoleted a great many parts for vintage Fords, these part numbers don't always exist in present-day dealer microfilms. This is called "NR" or "not replaced," which means it is no longer available from Ford. However, casting numbers on parts tell us a lot about the part.

Here's how a typical Ford part/casting number breaks down:
- First Position Indicates the **Decade**: (**C**5AE-6015-A)
  - B = 1950-59
  - C = 1960-69
  - D = 1970-79
  - E = 1980-89
  - F = 1990-99

- Second Position Indicates the **Year of Decade**: (C**5**AE-6015-A)

- Third Position Indicates the **Car Line**: (C5**A**E-6015-A)
  - A = Ford
  - D = Falcon

- G = Comet, Montego, Cyclone
- J = Marine and Industrial
- M = Mercury
- O = Fairlane and Torino
- S = Thunderbird
- T = Ford Truck
- V = Lincoln
- W = Cougar
- Z = Mustang

- Fourth Position Indicates the **Engineering Group**: (C5A**E**-6015-A)
  - A = Chassis Group
  - B = Body Group
  - E = Engine Group

If the item is a service part, the fourth position then indicates the applicable division as follows.
  - Z = Ford Division
  - Y = Lincoln-Mercury
  - X = Original Ford Muscle Parts Program
  - M = Ford Motorsport SVO or Ford-Mexico

- Four-Digit Number Indicates the **Basic Part Number**: (C5AE-**6015**-A)
  The basic part number tells us what the basic part is. For example, "6015" in the example above is a cylinder block. The number "9510" is carburetors, and so on. Each type of Ford part, right down to brackets and hardware, has a basic part number. This makes finding them easier in the Ford Master Parts Catalog.

- The last character (C5AE-6015-**A**) is the Suffix.
  The suffix indicates the revision under the part number. "A" indicates an original part. "B" indicates first revision, "C" second revision, "D" third revision, and so on. During Ford's learning curve with emissions in the 1970s, it was not uncommon to see "AA," "AB," and so on in cylinder-head casting suffix codes.

DATE CODES

Date codes can be found two ways in Ford castings. When the four-character date code is cast into the piece, this indicates when it was cast at the foundry. When it is stamped into the piece, this indicates the date of manufacture.

5 A 26
Year (5)/Month (A)/ Day (26)

TYPICAL DATE CODE

Another area of interest to Ford buffs is where the piece was cast or forged. With Ford engines, we've seen three foundry identification marks. A "C" circled around an "F" indicates the Cleveland Iron Foundry. "DIF" indicates Dearborn Iron Foundry. "WF" or "WIF" indicates Windsor Iron Foundry. Single- and double-digit numbers typically indicate cavity numbers in the mold.

Ford Casting Identification (continued)

WORKBENCH TIP

"5D19" is the casting date code, which tells us April 19, 1965. The "65" is nothing more than the model year, readable at a glance.

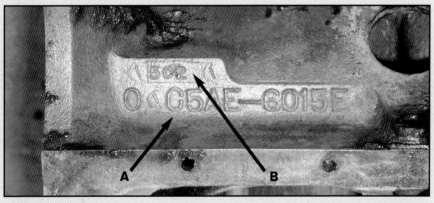

This is the casting number, which isn't always the same as the Ford part number. The casting number (A) indicates the engineering year involved. The date code (B) indicates the actual date of casting.

The manufacture date code is stamped in this boss at the front of the block. This tells us when the engine was assembled – "5C4" – March 4, 1965. Because the cylinder head just mentioned came off of this 289 engine, this tells us the cylinder head is a replacement casting, cast after the engine's original manufacture date.

Whenever you're shopping cylinder heads for a 289/302-ci engine, you will want early 289 castings with the pushrod guides cast into the cylinder head. This means using a cylinder head casting prior to April/May of 1966. Look for the pushrod guide holes in the head. From May 1966 and up, the pushrod hole is round and completely clears the pushrod. If you have no choice but to use heads designed for rail-style rocker arms, opt for pushrod guide plates with screw-in rocker-arm studs. If your budget doesn't permit this, find a set of 1962 to early 1966 castings.

Another cylinder head engineering change came in 1968 – the positive-stop rocker-arm stud, used in conjunction with the rail-style rocker arm. Positive-stop rocker arm studs are a "tighten it up and forget it" type. They are not adjustable.

Other considerations when choosing small-block Ford heads are combustion chamber size, port size, and valve size. When it comes to the 289- and 302-ci engines, port sizes never changed, nor did valve size. Contrary to all of the bench racing you've heard through the years, the 289 High Performance cylinder head does not have larger valves and ports. Combustion chamber size isn't any different from the 2V and 4V head either.

If you desire a smaller chamber and greater compression, opt for the 1968 302-4V head with the smaller 53-cc chamber. It's the only small-block Ford head that had a smaller chamber. The only exception to this statement is the 1962 to '64 221- and 260-ci heads, which had smaller 45- to 51-cc chambers. They also had smaller ports and valve sizes, which makes them a poor choice if you're interested in power. The 1968 302-4V head is a good factory cylinder head if you're interested in improved low-end torque with a basically stock 289/302-ci engine. However, it is a very difficult cylinder head to find because it was cast for one year only.

Small-block Ford cylinder heads began to change significantly in the 1970s, which is where you need to pay even closer attention to casting differences. Port and valve sizes remain virtually the same

IMPORTANT STEP !

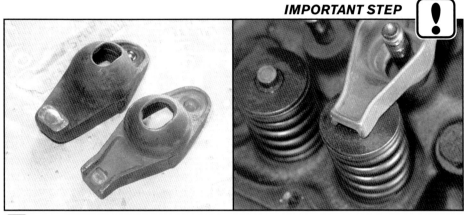

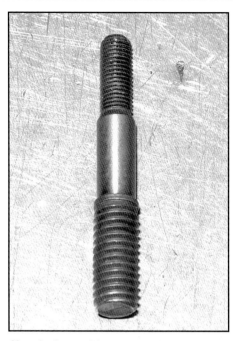

Here are the two types of rocker arms used on small-block Fords prior to 1978. On the left is the 1962 through early 1966 rocker arm used on cylinder heads with the pushrod guide cast into the head. On the right is the rail-style rocker arm used from May 8, 1966, through 1977. The rail-style rocker arm, as its name implies, has rails around the valvestem, which keeps the rocker arm centered on the valvestem. This idea saved Ford lots of money in machining costs and simplified design. However, do not use this rocker arm configuration with a high-performance camshaft.

Here is the positive-stop rocker-arm stud, which entered production in 1968. Just crank this one down tight and forget it.

Another point to remember with conventional versus rail-style rocker arms is valvestem tip length. Rail-style rocker arms have a longer valvestem tip than conventional rocker arms. It is a good idea to use the short stem with conventional rocker arms and the long tip with rail-style. Never use the rail-style rocker arm with the short-stem valves.

This is the bolt-fulcrum rocker-arm design that entered small-block production in 1978. It is a no-adjust rocker arm designed only for use with mild camshafts and hydraulic lifters. This design first entered production on the 351 Cleveland middle-block and 429/460-ci big-blocks. It took a decade for it to find use on the small-block Ford.

This is typical of an early small-block Ford head with smaller 53–57-cc chambers. The very early 221/260 head has even smaller chambers.

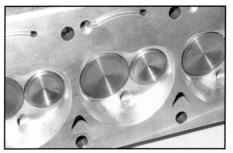

Here's a larger 64-cc chamber in an aluminum aftermarket cylinder head. Chamber size affects compression ratio. Aluminum enables you to run more compression because it gets rid of heat more quickly.

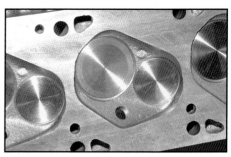

This is a 351C-4V wedge chamber, which yields an 11.0:1 compression stock. The 351C-2V chamber is an "open" chamber designed to yield less compression. However, the 2V head is more prone to detonation. It's a tough head to recommend. The 4V head is less prone to detonation, but its huge ports make it impractical for street use.

The 351C-4V head offers much larger intake and exhaust ports, but it doesn't do anything for the low-end torque you need on the street. This cylinder head is happiest at 7,000 rpm. Consider the Australian 351C head, which is a nice combination of conservative 2V port sizing and the 351C-4V wedge chamber. It is the perfect street head for any 351C project.

for 289/302 heads through the years, but combustion chamber changes a lot after 1971. You guessed it – the chamber sizes got larger. When combustion chamber size increases, compression drops. Ford, as well as all of the U.S. automakers, dropped compression to both improve emissions and deal with steadily falling octane ratings at the time. Beginning in 1975, Ford went with hardened exhaust valve seats for more reliable performance with low-lead and no-lead fuels.

When you are building a small-block Ford with flat-top pistons, you can cheat a little on chamber size, but when chamber size grows to 64cc and beyond, your engine will suffer significant losses in compression – and power. With a 53- to 57-cc chamber and a flat-top piston, you can expect a compression ratio of about 10.5:1 depending on compression height. This is where you

really have to do your homework in the planning process. You don't want to discover you have too much compression, or too little, when the engine is assembled. Check out the Engine Math chapter information on how to precisely calculate your compression ratio.

Beginning in 1978, the small-block Ford cylinder head took on the same rocker-arm set-up as the 351C, 351M, 400M, and the 385-series 429/460-ci big-blocks. Instead of the ball-stud rocker-arm setup the small-block Ford had always had, the 1978 and later head has the bolt-fulcrum, stamped-steel, non-adjustable rocker arm. As in 1968, just tighten it up and forget it. This approach works well with stock applications. It does not work well with aggressive aftermarket camshafts, which will tend to beat the stock rockers to pieces. Aggressive aftermarket camshafts call

for screw-in studs and adjustable rocker arms. This is a modification your machine shop can handle.

Another path to power is cylinder-head porting. Head porting is an art that takes years of practice and experience to refine. Our friend, John Da Luz of JMC Motorsports, understands how to make the most of a cylinder head. He has experimented with dozens of Ford cylinder-head castings over the years. The result is 289/302 head castings that flow well in excess of 200 cfm on the intake side, which is on a par with some of the aftermarket heads out there. A set of these heads will wake up your low-displacement small-block.

John tells us it's a matter of understanding port dynamics. Small-block Fords, for example, suffer not so much from small intake ports, but small exhaust ports that do not scavenge well. John's porting technique removes the thermactor "hump" (all small-block Ford heads have them, even 49-state heads), opens up the port, and smooths out exhaust flow into the header. This port/gasket match-porting job is economical and will yield lots of power. A full-blown porting job and larger valves will give you torque you never dreamed of from a stock head. As a proven engine builder, John can advise you on the best course of action for your small-block Ford

351W CYLINDER HEADS

Before the aftermarket really took off, small-block Ford buffs looked to the 351W cylinder head for power improvements. The 351W head gives the 289/302 plenty of breathability with its larger intake and exhaust ports and larger valves. If you port the 351W head, it only gets better. However, if you're going to go through the expense of port and bowl work on 351W heads, which can run as high as $1,000, you might as well go with good aftermarket aluminum heads instead. Right out of the

Small-Block Cylinder-Head Identification

Here's a helpful chart that I put together to help you identify and locate all kinds of Ford factory cylinder heads.

Displacement/Year	Casting Number	Chamber Size	Valve Size	Port Size
221-ci (1962-63)	C2OE-A	45-51 cc	1.59" Int.	1.76" x 1.00" Intake
	C2OE-B	45-51 cc	1.39" Exh.	1.24" x 1.00" Exhaust
	C2OE-C	45-51 cc		
	C2OE-D	45-51 cc		
	C2OE-E	45-51 cc		
	C3OE-A	45-51 cc		
255-ci (1980-81)	EOSE-AB	53.6-56cc	1.68" Int.	N/A
			1.46" Exh.	N/A
260-ci (1962-63)	C2OE-F	52-55 cc	1.59" Int.	1.76" x 1.00" Intake
	C3OE-B	52-55 cc	1.39" Exh.	1.24" x 1.00" Exhaust
260-ci (1964)	C4OE-B (1964)	52-55 cc	1.67" Int.	1.76" x 1.00" Intake
	Revised 260 Head		1.45" Exh.	1.24" x 1.00" Exhaust
289-ci (1963-67)	C3AE-F	52-55 cc	1.78" Int.	1.94" x 1.04" Intake
	C3OE-E	52-55 cc	1.45" Exh.	
	C3OE-F	52-55 cc		
	C4AE-C	52-55 cc		
	C5DE-B	52-55 cc		
	C6DE-G	52-55 cc		
	C6OE-C	52-55 cc	1.78" Int.	1.94" x 1.04" Intake
	(Thermactor)		1.45" Exh.	1.24" x 1.00" Exhaust
	C6OE-E	52-55 cc	1.78" Int.	1.94" x 1.04" Intake
	(Thermactor)		1.45" Exh.	1.24" x 1.00" Exhaust
	C6OE-M	63 cc	1.78" Int.	1.94" x 1.04" Intake
	C7OE-A (Thermactor)	63 cc	1.45" Exh.	1.24" x 1.00" Exhaust
	C7OE-B	63 cc	1.78" Int.	1.94" x 1.04" Intake
	(Thermactor)		1.45" Exh.	1.24" x 1.00" Exhaust
	C7OE-C	63 cc	1.78" Int.	1.94" x 1.04" Intake
	C7OZ-B	63 cc	1.45" Exh.	1.24" x 1.00" Exhaust
	(Thermactor)			
	C7ZE-A	63 cc	1.78" Int.	1.94" x 1.04" Intake
	(Thermactor)		1.45" Exh.	1.24" x 1.00" Exhaust
	C8OE-D	63 cc	1.78" Int.	1.94" x 1.04" Intake
	(Thermactor)		1.45" Exh.	1.24" x 1.00" Exhaust

(continued)

Small-Block Cylinder-Head Identification (continued)

Displacement/Year	Casting Number	Chamber Size	Valve Size	Port Size
289-ci (1963-67) (continued)	C8OE-L (Thermactor)	63 cc	1.78" Int. 1.45" Exh.	1.94" x 1.04" Intake 1.24" x 1.00" Exhaust
	C8OE-M (Thermactor)	63 cc	1.78" Int. 1.45" Exh.	1.94" x 1.04" Intake 1.24" x 1.00" Exhaust
289-ci (1963-67) High Performance	C3OE C4OE-B C5OE-A C5AE-E	52-55 cc 52-55 cc 52-55 cc 52-55 cc	1.78" Int. 1.45" Exh.	1.94" x 1.04" Intake 1.24" x 1.00" Exhaust
Service Head	C7ZZ-B (Part No.)	52-55 cc	1.78" Int. 1.45" Exh.	1.94" x 1.04" Intake 1.24" x 1.00" Exhaust
302-ci (1968-78)	C7OE-C C7OE-G C8OE-F (4V Head) C8OE-J	63 cc 63 cc 53.5 cc 63 cc	1.78" Int. 1.45" Exh.	1.94" x 1.04" Intake 1.24" x 1.00" Exhaust
	C8OE-K (Thermactor)	58.2 cc	1.78" Int. 1.45" Exh.	1.94" x 1.04" Intake 1.24" x 1.00" Exhaust
	C8OE-L (Thermactor)	58.2 cc	1.78" Int. 1.45" Exh.	1.94" x 1.04" Intake 1.24" x 1.00" Exhaust
	C8OE-M C8AE-J C8DE-F	63 cc 63 cc 63 cc	1.78" Int. 1.45" Exh.	1.94" x 1.04" Intake 1.24" x 1.00" Exhaust
	C9TE-C (Truck Head)	69 cc	1.78" Int. 1.45" Exh.	1.94" x 1.04" Intake 1.24" x 1.00" Exhaust
	D0OE-B	N/A	1.78" Int. 1.45" Exh.	1.94" x 1.04" Intake 1.24" x 1.00" Exhaust
	D1TZ-A (Truck Head)	N/A	1.78" Int. 1.45" Exh.	1.94" x 1.04" Intake 1.24" x 1.00" Exhaust
	D2OE-BA D5OE-GA D5OE-A3A D5OE-A3B D7OE-DA D8OE-AB	N/A	1.78" Int. 1.45" Exh.	1.94" x 1.04" Intake 1.24" x 1.00" Exhaust
302-ci 1979-84	D9AE-AA	67.5-70 cc	1.78" Int. 1.46" Exh.	1.94" x 1.04" Intake 1.24" x 1.00" Exhaust
302-ci 1985 High Output	E5AE-CA	67-70 cc	1.78" Int. 1.46" Exh.	1.94" x 1.04" Intake 1.24" x 1.00" Exhaust
302-ci 1986 High Output	E6AE-AA	62-65 cc	1.78" Int. 1.46" Exh.	1.94" x 1.04" Intake 1.24" x 1.00" Exhaust
302-ci 1987-93	E5TE-PA E7TE-PA	62-65 cc	1.78" Int. 1.46" Exh.	1.94" x 1.04" Intake 1.24" x 1.00" Exhaust

(continued)

Small-Block Cylinder-Head Identification (continued)

Displacement/Year	Casting Number	Chamber Size	Valve Size	Port Size
302-ci (1993) Cobra	F3ZE-AA	60-63 cc	1.84" Int. 1.54" Exh.	N/A
302-ci (1994-95) Cobra	F4ZE-AA	60-63 cc	1.84" Int. 1.54" Exh.	N/A
302-ci (1996-97) Explorer	F1ZE-AA	63-66 cc	1.84" Int. 1.46" Exh.	N/A
302-ci (1997-2000) Explorer	F7ZE-AA	58-61 cc	1.84" Int. 1.46" Exh.	N/A
302-ci (1969-70) Boss 302	C9ZE-A	61-64 cc	2.23" Int.	2.50" x 1.75" Intake
	C9ZE-C	61-64 cc	1.71" Exh.	2.00" x 1.74" Exhaust
	D0ZE-A	58 cc	2.19" Int.	2.50" x 1.75" Intake
	D1ZE-A	58 cc	1.71" Exh.	2.00" x 1.74" Exhaust
351W (1969-84)	C9OE-B	60 cc	1.84" Int.	1.94" x 1.76" Intake
	C9OE-D	60 cc	1.54" Exh.	1.24" x 1.00" Exhaust
	D0OE-C	60 cc		
	D0OE-G	60 cc		
	D5TE-EB	69 cc	1.78" Int.	1.94" x 1.04" Intake
	(Truck Head)	69 cc	1.45" Exh.	1.24" x 1.00" Exhaust
	D7OE-A	69 cc	1.78" Int.	1.94" x 1.04" Intake
	D8OE-A	69 cc	1.45" Exh.	1.24" x 1.00" Exhaust
	D8OE-AB	69 cc		
351W (1985-86)	E5AE-CA	67-70 cc	1.78" Int. 1.45" Exh.	1.94" x 1.04" Intake 1.24" x 1.00" Exhaust
351W (1987-95)	E7TE-PA	62-65 cc	1.78" Int. 1.45" Exh.	1.94" x 1.04" Intake 1.24" x 1.00" Exhaust

box, aftermarket aluminum heads outflow and outperform the stock 351W head casting, even with port and bowl work. If you are looking for cheap, bolt-on power, go with 351W heads and leave the ports alone.

The most important issue to remember about 351W heads is which ones were just 302 heads on top of the 351W block. Beginning in the mid 1970s (1975 for truck castings and 1977 for cars), the 351W was fitted with 302 cylinder-head castings – which means port and valve sizes that aren't any different. Avoid this casting because it won't make any difference in power. If anything, it will make less power. The best 351W head castings were produced from 1969 to '74, with right-sized chambers, ports, and valves for the 289/302.

AFTERMARKET CYLINDER HEADS

If you're seeking an aggressive camshaft and 400 horsepower, stock cylinder heads probably won't be your casting of choice. You're going to want to go with good aftermarket cylinder heads that outflow the stock pieces and weigh less. Any time you're going to go through the expense of aftermarket

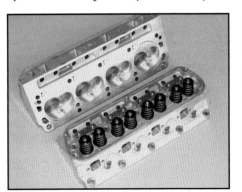 

The Edelbrock Performer RPM cylinder head is a nice upgrade for small-block Fords. For around $1,200, you can improve airflow, raise compression, and boost power with a pair of Performer RPM heads. Aluminum heads conduct and carry heat better than iron heads. They also weigh less. If you are bolting these heads on an older small-block 289 or 302, be mindful of the larger chambers, which will reduce compression dramatically.

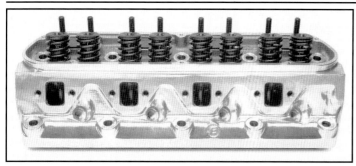

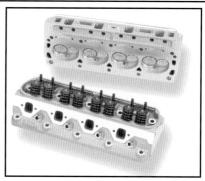

Holley has struggled to get on the cylinder head bandwagon and be noticed by performance buffs. However, Holley is making strides, and better cylinder heads, these days. These heads are made of 356-T6 aluminum, have "right-sized" intake and exhaust runners, heavy-duty valvesprings and retainers, and are CNC-machined for accuracy.

If you happen to be building a stroker, the Edelbrock Victor Jr. is a better head for greater displacements. This is also a good cylinder head for high-revving, low-displacement small-blocks that need generous breathing. Again, remember chamber size and how it affects compression ratio. Check out my factory and aftermarket cylinder head charts for all the info.

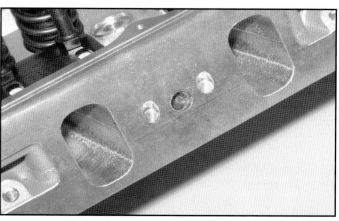

This is the AFR 165 cylinder head – the perfect street head for just about any small-block Ford. If you're going to raise displacement, the AFR 185, with 2.02/1.60-inch valves may be a better choice. Much depends on piston-to-valve clearance issues. Each of the AFR cylinder heads delivers consistently better performance through its CNC-machined ports and chambers. AFR is a cylinder head company we feel quite comfortable with.

cylinder heads, they probably won't be iron, either.

Aftermarket aluminum heads serve a valuable purpose in so many ways. First, they flow better. Second, they weigh less than iron. Third, they dissipate heat better than iron, which means you can run a higher compression ratio without getting into trouble. These are three very good reasons to go with aftermarket aluminum heads.

We get more power from our small-block Ford by increasing the compression ratio. However, with compression come higher combustion temperatures and pressures. Because aluminum is a great conductor of heat, it carries excessive heat away from the combustion chamber. This means we can push our engine a little harder with a higher compression ratio, nitrous, or supercharging.

Of all the aftermarket cylinder heads we've seen, AFR heads appear to be the best bang for the buck because they flow so well and yield more power. Right in the same ballpark as the AFR head are Trick Flow heads, which do a

Guide to Ford Aftermarket Cylinder Heads

If you decide you want to make a little more power than the factory heads can provide, you might be able to find what you need in this chart.

Manufacturer	Type/Number	Intake Valve	Exhaust Valve	Chamber
AFR	Street 165 cc	1.90"	1.60"	58 or 61 cc
AFR	Street/Strip 165 cc	1.90"	1.60"	58 or 61 cc
AFR	Street 185 cc	2.02"	1.60"	58 or 61 cc
AFR	Street/Strip 185 cc	2.02"	1.60"	58 or 61 cc
AFR	205 cc SBF Race Head	2.08"	1.60"	60 or 71 cc
AFR	225 cc SBF Race Head	2.08"	1.60"	60 cc
Edelbrock	Performer #60319 Bare #60329 Assembled	1.90"	1.60"	60 cc
Edelbrock	Performer #60349	2.02"	1.60"	60 cc
Edelbrock	Performer #60279 Assembled Loc-Wire	2.02"	1.60"	60 cc
Edelbrock	Performer #60219 Bare #60229 Assembled Non-Emissions	1.90"	1.60"	60 cc
Edelbrock	Performer RPM #60249 Bare #60259 Assembled Non-Emissions	2.02"	1.60"	60 cc
Edelbrock	Performer RPM #60259 Assembled Loc-Wire	2.02"	1.60"	60 cc
Edelbrock	Performer RPM #602159 Polished	2.02"	1.60"	60 cc
Edelbrock	Performer RPM 5.0L/5.8L #60369 Bare #60379 Assembled	1.90"	1.60"	60 cc
Edelbrock	Performer RPM 5.0L/5.8L #60289 Assembled Loc-Wire	1.90"	1.60"	60 cc
Edelbrock	Performer RPM 5.0L/5.8L #60389 Bare #60399 Assembled	2.02"	1.60"	60 cc
Edelbrock	Performer RPM 5.0L/5.8L #60299 Assembled Loc-Wire	2.02"	1.60"	60 cc

(continued)

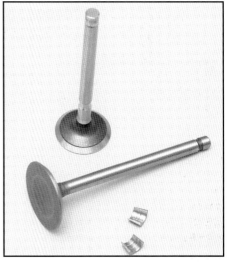

Every engine rebuild should include new valves. This helps ensure rebuild integrity by allowing you to begin with fresh valve faces and stems. To save money, you can reface old valves and clean up the valvestems. But, you will never get these surfaces as true as they are new. And remember, most engine failures are caused by some sort of valvetrain mishap.

pretty good job on small-block Fords. The rest of the market, Edelbrock, Ford Racing, and World Products have good cylinder head castings for the money, but few of them perform as well as AFR and Trick Flow on the flow bench and in the dyno room. You need to stay tuned, because the marketplace is ever changing. New cylinder-head castings are showing up all the time from these manufacturers. This competition in the cylinder-head market is good news for you, beating a path to your door with better mousetraps all the time.

The main issue to keep in mind with aftermarket cylinder heads is compatibility with existing stuff. More than one of us has purchased aftermarket cylinder heads, only to discover they aren't compatible with the headers and exhaust systems we already have. This is especially true with raised-port and high-port heads. This is also counter-productive when you're trying to make power for less money. Cylinder head manufacturers are working harder to improve exhaust system compatibility, but there are still plenty of examples out there in the marketplace that won't work with your Hooker Super Comps

Guide to Ford Aftermarket Cylinder Heads (continued)

Manufacturer	Type/Number	Intake Valve	Exhaust Valve	Chamber
Edelbrock	Victor Jr. #77169 Bare #77179 with valves only #77189 with valves, springs and keepers #77199 with valves, springs, and keepers for mechanical roller cams	2.05"	1.60"	60 cc
Edelbrock	Victor Jr. #77389 Bare	2.05"	1.60"	70 cc
Edelbrock	Victor Jr. CNC #61269 Bare Std. Exhaust Pattern	2.10"	1.60"	60 cc
Edelbrock	Victor Jr. CNC #61279 Bare J302 Pattern	2.10"	1.60"	60 cc
Edelbrock	Glidden Victor CNC #61099 Bare	N/A	N/A	56 cc
Edelbrock	Glidden Victor CNC #77099 Bare For 9.2" Blocks with 9.5" manifold.			56 cc
Edelbrock	Victor Ford #77219 Bare	N/A	N/A	47 cc
Edelbrock	Chapman Victor CNC 276 cc Head #61299 Bare	N/A	N/A	60 cc
Edelbrock	Chapman Victor CNC 255 cc Head #77289 Bare	N/A	N/A	50 cc
Edelbrock	Chapman Victor CNC 255 cc Head #77299	N/A	N/A	61 cc
Ford	GT-40 "Turbo-Swirl" Aluminum M-6049-Y302 (Bare Head) M-6049-Y303 (Complete)	1.94"	1.60"	64 cc
Ford	GT-40X "Turbo-Swirl" Aluminum M-6049-X302 (Bare Head) M-6049-X303 (Complete)	1.94"	1.54"	64 cc

(continued)

or Shelby Tri-Ys. This is where it gets expensive. When you're shopping for aftermarket cylinder heads, ask the manufacturer about header and exhaust system compatibility.

CRANKSHAFTS

Ford utilized surprisingly few crankshaft types in its small-block engines. The 221-, 260-, and 289-ci engines all used the same cast-iron crankshaft, making this crank widely available for three different displacements. This crankshaft is identified with a "1M" in the front journal area. While it's easy to assume the 289 High Performance engine had the same type of forged-steel crankshaft also used in the 1969 to '70 Boss 302 engine that came years later, exactly the opposite is true. The 289 High Performance engine used the same 1M cast-iron crank as the 289-2V and 4V engines – with the exception that it was Brinell tested for toughness and was supported with wider main bearing caps. It was not a high-nodular iron crank, but simply a hand-picked, standard nodular iron crank. If your faith in this crankshaft is lacking, con-

When it's time to choose a camshaft and valvetrain, it must be a package deal, with valvesprings and a cam profile that are suited to one another. Really stiff valvesprings with a mild lobe profile will wipe the cam lobe. Springs that aren't stiff enough for the lobe profile will cause valve float at high revs. Whenever you purchase a set of aftermarket cylinder heads, never trust the valvesprings and valves that come with the head. Check each and every valve and spring before the head goes on your engine. Chances are good you'll need a different valvespring for your camshaft application.

Guide to Ford Aftermarket Cylinder Heads (continued)

Manufacturer	Type/Number	Intake Valve	Exhaust Valve	Chamber
Ford	GT-40X "Turbo-Swirl" Aluminum M-6049-X304 (Bare Head)	1.94"	1.54"	58 cc
	M-6049-X305 (Complete)			
Ford	Sportsman Short Track Cast Iron M-6049-N351	2.02"	1.60"	64 cc
Ford	"Z" Head Aluminum	2.02"	1.60"	64 cc
Holley	300-551-2 Pedestal Mount	1.90"	1.60"	63 cc
Holley	300-573 Stud Mount	1.90"	1.60"	63 cc
Holley	300-574 Pedestal Mount	2.02"	1.60"	63 cc
Holley	300-575 Stud Mount	2.02"	1.60"	63 cc
Trick Flow	Twisted Wedge Aluminum TFS-51400002	2.02"	1.60"	61 cc
Trick Flow	Twisted Wedge Aluminum TFS-51400003	2.02"	1.60"	61 cc
Trick Flow	Track Heat Aluminum TFS-52400010	2.02"	1.60"	61 cc
Trick Flow	Track Heat Aluminum TFS-52400011	2.02"	1.60"	61 cc
Trick Flow	R-Series Aluminum TFS-52400001	2.08"	1.60"	61 cc
Trick Flow	R-Series Aluminum TFS-52400101	2.08"	1.60"	61 cc
Trick Flow	R-Series Aluminum TFS-52400201	2.08"	1.60"	61 cc
Trick Flow	R-Series Aluminum TFS-52400100	2.08"	1.60"	61 cc
Trick Flow	R-Series Aluminum TFS-52400200	2.08"	1.60"	61 cc
Trick Flow	High Port Aluminum TFS-51700001	2.02"	1.60"	64 cc
Trick Flow	High Port Aluminum TFS-51700002	2.02"	1.60"	64 cc

(continued)

Here's a double valvespring for use with an aggressive camshaft. We go with the double spring for greater pressure in order to snap the valve closed more quickly at high RPM.

This is a Crane valvespring with a dampener for stability. It's a mild spring designed for use with a less-aggressive profile.

sider this: Carroll Shelby and his team went racing in SCCA competition, winding this crankshaft to 8,000 rpm, beating Corvettes in the process. With some shotpeening and nitriding, you can trust this crankshaft in your weekend drag racer.

The 289 High Performance crankshaft is also identified by the same 1M

Guide to Ford Aftermarket Cylinder Heads (continued)

Manufacturer	Type/Number	Intake Valve	Exhaust Valve	Chamber
World Products	Windsor Jr. Cast Iron 053030 Bar	1.94"	1.60"	58 cc
World Products	Windsor Jr. Cast Iron 053030-1 (Hydraulic	1.94"	1.60"	58 cc
World Products	Windsor Jr. Cast Iron 053030-2 (Hydraulic Roller)	1.94"	1.60"	58 cc
World Products	Windsor Jr. Cast Iron 053030-3 (Solid Roller)	1.94"	1.60"	58 cc
World Products	Windsor Jr. Lite Aluminum 023030 (Bare)	1.94"	1.60"	58 cc
World Products	Windsor Jr. Lite Aluminum 023030-2 (Hydraulic Roller)	1.94"	1.60"	58 cc
World Products	Windsor Jr. Lite 023030-3 (Solid Roller)	1.94"	1.60"	58 cc
World Products	Windsor Sr. Lite Aluminum 023020 (Bare)	2.02"	1.60"	64 cc
World Products	Windsor Sr. Lite Aluminum 023020-2 (Hydraulic Roller)	2.02"	1.60"	64 cc
World Products	Windsor Sr. Lite Aluminum 023020-3 (Solid Roller)	2.02"	1.60"	64 cc
World Products	Roush 200 Cast Iron 053040 (Bare)	2.02"	1.60"	64 cc
World Products	Roush 200 Cast Iron 053040-1 (Hydraulic)	2.02"	1.60"	64 cc
World Products	Roush 200 Cast Iron 053040-2 (Hydraulic Roller)	2.02"	1.60"	64 cc
World Products	Roush 200 Cast Iron 053040-3 (Solid Roller)	2.02"	1.60"	64 cc

casting number, sometimes with a letter "K" or a Brinell test mark stamped nearby. Dimensionally, the 289 High Performance crankshaft is exactly the same as the standard crank, with a 2.87-inch stroke. Care must be exercised in this regard because it is easy to fake a 289 High Performance crankshaft by simply adding the "K" or Brinell test mark to a standard crankshaft.

The 302's cast-iron crankshaft, first available in 1968, is identified with a "2M" cast into the forward-most counterweight. Newer 5.0-liter crankshafts are identified with a "2MA" on the journal. Beginning in 1985, Ford went to a one-piece rear main seal, which eliminates the seal lip found on the older 221/260/289/302 crank. The 2M crank is not interchangeable with the 221, 260, and 289 connecting rods and pistons.

The Boss 302 crankshaft mentioned earlier can be identified by its forged steel design. It can also be identified by either a D0ZE-A or TFE-8 marking on the crankshaft journal. Because Boss 302 crankshafts are so rare, it is unlikely you will stumble upon one cheap at a swap meet. Plus, you really want the whole Boss 302 package. What's the point of building a two-bolt main small-block with a Boss 302 crankshaft? Ideally, you will find the entire engine and do some dream spinning with your machine shop.

The 351W cast iron crankshaft is easy to identify by observing the "3M" on the forward-most counterweight. It also has larger main journals than the 1M or 2M crankshafts. A forged-steel crankshaft was never available from the factory for the 351W. Like the 302 crank, the 351W went to a one-piece seal in 1985, just like the 302, eliminating the lip and leaky two-piece seal.

The 351C, 351M, and 400M are still considered by Ford as small-blocks. Chevrolet did a 400-ci small-block designed mostly for truck applications. It was lightweight and packed a lot of torque, thanks to its long stroke. We tend to call the 351 Cleveland, and its larger siblings, the 351M and 400M, "middle-blocks," because they really aren't small-block engines at all. They're heavier, for one thing. For another, their only selling point was their great-flow-

When we get into aftermarket rocker arms, they range from stock iron to stamped steel to cast and forged aluminum. This is an entry-level stamped-steel, roller-tip rocker arm from Lunati Cams. Use this kind of rocker arm with a mild cam profile. There's less friction thanks to the roller tip. It is also stronger than a stock cast iron rocker arm.

This is an entry-level stamped-steel rocker arm from Lunati Cams for 1978-up Ford heads with bolt-fulcrum rocker arms.

ing, big-port cylinder heads. The 351C, produced from 1970 to '74, is rather scarce these days. The 400M, a tall-deck version of the Cleveland introduced in 1972, was destroked to 351 ci in 1975 to make the 351M. This made it cheaper for Ford to produce two displacements using one block casting.

One thing the 351C, 351M, and 400M have in common is that they used a cast-iron crankshaft in all applications. Standard 351C cranks are marked "4M" and sport a 3.50-inch stroke. Boss 351 (1971) and 351 High Output (1972) cranks are marked "4MA" and are Brinell tested for the same reasons as the 289 High Performance crankshaft. A 351M can be stroked to 400 ci by installing a 400M crank. The 351C can be stroked by modifying and installing a 400M crankshaft. This modification is good for well in excess of 400 ci in the super-tough Cleveland.

STROKER CRANKS

It is much easier to build power into your small-block Ford today, thanks to the huge array of stroker kits available for small-block Fords. You can build a

---

Stroker Kits

WORKBENCH TIP

Since I've already covered stroker kits extensively in *How To Build Big-Inch Ford Small-Blocks*, I'm just going to give you a quick rundown to help you make educated decisions in your small-block build.

Stroker kits are a great way to bolt in horsepower and torque, and they don't cost much more than a regular rebuild. By choosing a crankshaft with a longer stroke, you can add cubic inches, and power, to your small-block Ford. Before you even consider building a stroker small-block, ask yourself how much power you need for your application. If you are building a weekend pleasure cruiser, you don't need to turn your 302 into a 347-ci stroker. However, maybe you are building a 351W for your pick-up truck that's going to do a lot of towing. A 408-ci stroker will make you plenty of good low- and mid-range torque for towing. Perhaps you are building a Saturday-night special for the drag strip; a stroker can help you there, too.

Once you have determined how you're going to approach your small-block project, you can move ahead and purchase a kit and have the machine work done. When you're considering a stroker kit, we suggest choosing something on the conservative side – such as a 331-ci kit for a 302 or a 393-ci kit for your 351W. This keeps you from getting near your engine's limit. You can make all kinds of torque with a 393 or 408 without nearing the 351W's 429-ci design limits. Going with a 392 or 408 allows your engine to live longer and more reliably.

You can even push the cubes skyward in your 351C with a 408-ci stroker kit from Speed-O-Motive. You can make some good, affordable torque

from a relatively stock small-block. Most of the more conservative stroker kits are little more than Ford parts machined specially to give you some extra cubic inches. Sometimes, a stroker kit might even use Chrysler or Chevrolet rods in order to get the configuration to work.

Stroker kits become expensive when our expectations get lofty. For example, do you intend to push your small-block hard? Do you really need a steel crank and H-beam rods? Do you really need forged pistons? If you just need good, healthy torque, find contentment in a budget stroker kit with a proven reputation. Check around and see who makes the best kits at affordable prices. There are enough companies out there making these kits, which means you have the benefit of competition in the marketplace.

221/260/289/302/351W/Boss 302 Crankshaft Identification

Displacement/Year	Casting/Forging Number	Stroke/Other Information
221-ci (1962-63)	C2OZ, C3OZ	2.87" Also marked 1M
260ci (1962-64)	C2OZ, C3OZ	2.87" Also marked 1M
289-ci (1963-67)	C3OZ	2.87 Also marked 1M
289-ci (1963-67) High Performance	C3OZ	2.87" Brinell test mark on journal. Also marked 1M. Some cranks are falsely Brinell test marked. Watch for fakes.
302-ci (1968-81)	C8AZ-A	3.00" Also marked 2M
302-ci (1978-up)	E0SE-AD	3.00" Lincoln Versailles crank designed for EEC-I system
351W (1969-72)	No Casting Number	3.50" Marked 3M or 3C
351W (1973-up)	No Casting Number	3.50" Marked 3MA
302-ci (1969-70) Boss 302	D0ZE-A	3.00" Also marked 7FE-8 Forged steel crankshaft

351C/351M/400M Crankshaft Identification

Displacement/Year	Casting Number	Stroke/Other Information
351C (1970-74)	No Casting Number	3.50" Marked 4M
351C (1971) Boss 351	No Casting Number	3.50" Brinell test mark on journal. Marked 4MA
351M (1975-80)	No Casting Number	3.50"
400M (1972-80)	No Casting Number	4.00"

higher-displacement stroker small-block for about the same amount of money you can build a 289/302/351W/351C. If you are seeking a low-buck increase in horsepower and torque, you may opt for a budget stroker kit from Performance Automotive Warehouse or Speed-O-Motive for about the same amount of money as a basic standard-inch build-up.

Affordable stroker kits use what's already available without expensive tooling costs. We get 400+ cubic inches from a 351W or 351C by machining a

400M crank down to size and dropping it in a 351-ci block. Fit the 400M crank into a 351W or 351C block and make 408 ci. The crank comes cheap because it's already there. Go to the Chrysler parts bin and opt for a set of 360-ci rods, then machine them to fit the 400M crank. Your Windsor or Cleveland powerhouse doesn't know the Chrysler rods are in there. Neither will your friends if you keep your mouth shut. Friends will notice when you dust off their doors on Airport Road or out at the drag strip.

We can build an affordable 289/302 stroker by using a 351W crank turned down to size to achieve 347 ci. A custom crank will get you anywhere from 331 to 355 ci depending on the kit you choose.

The stroker kit gets you into all kinds of power for less money. If you're hell-bent to pump even more cubes into your small-block, it becomes more expensive. A custom stroker kit with a steel crank and H-beam rods gets pricey. But if you're going to run nitrous or boost, a budget stroker kit will self-destruct the minute you throw some squeeze at it. Build for the power you intend to make. Do it on a budget, throw nitrous at it, and watch the parts fly. A cast crank and forged I-beam rods will not take a nitrous blast without complaint. They will fail – and require you to build another engine all over again.

CONNECTING RODS

Ford small-block engines have been blessed with rock-solid bottom ends from the factory for more than 40 years. The 221-, 260-, 289-, and 302-ci engines have strong forged-steel connecting rods that have undergone very few engineering changes throughout their production life. The 289 High Performance connecting rod, for example, differs little from the standard rod except for a larger 3/8-inch bolt pressed into a broached seat. Because connecting rod bolts are the single greatest reason for rod failure at high revs, the larger 3/8-inch bolt is a great deterrent to failure.

There are two basic small-block Ford connecting rods for 289/302 engines. The 221, 260, and 289 rod (5.1535 to 5.1565 inches center to center) is numbered "C3AE" while the 302 rod (5.0885 to 5.0915 inches center to center) is numbered "C8AE." The 302 connecting rod is actually shorter than the 221/260/289 rod. What may surprise you is the Boss 302 rod number "C3AE-D" is exactly the same rod forging as the C3AE with 3/8-inch bolts for structural integrity at high revs. When we closely examine the Boss 302 rod, the large end of this rod appears to be a bit beefier than its 289/302 counterpart, but the Boss 302 rod is basically nothing more

Rear Main Seal

WORKBENCH TIP

For the better part of its production life, the small-block Ford had a two-piece rear main crankshaft oil seal. This seal is common with the 221-, 260-, 289-, 302-ci engines from 1962 to '84. Beginning in 1985, Ford went to a large one-piece rear main seal, which is less likely to leak. It looks like an enlarged version of the front crankshaft oil seal located in the timing cover. Fel-Pro gives you a convenient seal installation tool with the seal, which makes installation a snap.

If you are committed to using an older block with the two-piece seal, stagger the seal gaps away from the main cap parting lines. Use a good silicone sealer at all parting lines to reduce the chances of leakage.

than the 289 High Performance rod. The 221, 260, 289, and Boss 302 connecting rod later found its way into the 2.3L OHC turbo 4-cylinders used in the T-Bird Turbo Coupe, Cougar XR-7 Turbo, Mustang GT Turbo, and the Capri RS Turbo available during the 1980s. There are a lot of them floating around out there.

Because the 302 has an entirely different bottom end dimensionally, it has the C8AE connecting rod forging married to its 2M crankshaft. This rod is not interchangeable with the 221/260/289 and Boss 302 engines just mentioned because it is shorter. The C8AE rod is common to all of the 302-ci (5.0L) engines. Aside from subtle improvements to this rod that came with the power increases of the 1980s, this rod is virtually the same and quite interchangeable. It's always wise to match a set of rods, which means a set of rods that are identical in appearance and forging numbers. One modification is upgrading the 302 rod bolt from 5/16 to 3/8 inch. This gives the 302 rod the durability of the 289 Hi-Po/Boss 302 rod mentioned earlier. One drawback here is rod integrity, because although larger bolts are stronger, we tend to weaken the rod when we take away some material to fit the larger bolt.

The 351W engine was equipped with one basic connecting rod, the C90Z unit with 3/8-inch bolts, regardless of the application. This rod has remained unchanged throughout the life of the 351W (and 5.8L).

The standard 351C-2V and 4V engines were fitted with the D0AZ-A rod forging. The Boss 351, not to mention the 351C High Output and CJ, were equipped with the D1ZX-AA connecting rod, which was Magnafluxed and shot-peened for added strength. This is a good thing to do with any small-block Ford connecting rod you intend to use. The 400M has a D1AZ-A rod that served with this engine throughout its entire production life.

Lunati Cams makes this forged-aluminum roller-rocker arm for more aggressive high-performance applications. This rocker tolerates a more radical cam profile and reduces some of that internal friction we were talking about in this chapter.

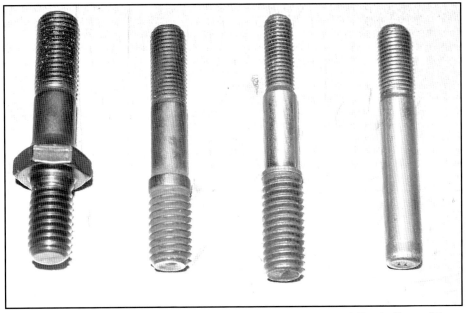

There are five basic types of rocker-arm studs used in small-block Fords. Four of them are shown here. From left to right: screw-in adjustable with hex head, screw-in adjustable without hex head, screw-in positive-stop, and press-in adjustable. Not shown is the press-in positive stop used from 1968 to '77.

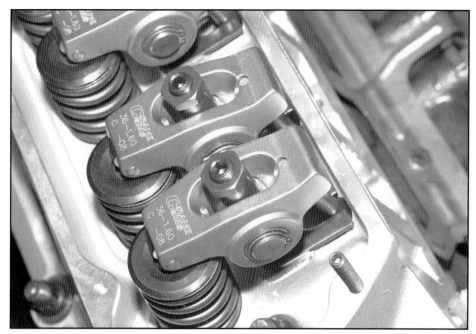

Shown here is the hex-head, screw-in rocker-arm stud, installed in an aftermarket aluminum head. Note the Crane adjustable roller rockers with a 1.60:1 ratio.

Connecting rod selection boils down to how you intend to use your engine. If you're going to lean on it periodically or are building a weekend cruiser, forged I-beam (stock) connecting rods are adequate. This means you can recondition your stock connecting rods, fit them with new ARP bolts, and be ahead of the game. You may also step up to larger 3/8-inch rod bolts for your 289/302 and have the integrity of a Boss 302 or 289 Hi-Po rod. Just remember to have the rod forgings shotpeened for added strength.

If you're going to blow squeeze at your 289/302/351, forged I-beam or H-beam rods become mandatory due to the loading they will see – even on a limited basis. The same can be said for supercharging or racing where the rods will be hammered hard on a regular basis.

Some drag racers use aluminum connecting rods, which are fine for drag racing but bad for road racing or street use. Aluminum rods weigh considerably less than their steel counterparts. This means they will consume less power. However, aluminum rods are appropriate only for the fast-quick blast of drag racing.

PISTONS

Whenever you're building an engine, thoughts always turn to piston selection. We told you in Chapter 1 that mission dictates how you should build your engine. If you're going to hammer it hard, you're going to need hypereutectic or forged pistons. If you're just going to do some weekend cruising, cast pistons are more than adequate.

Our 289 engine, which is being built by Jim Grubbs Motorsports in Valencia, California, is for a stock 1965 Mustang. This is an occasional driver that won't see much pedal time during its service life. As a result, we can easily get by with cheap, affordable cast pistons from Federal-Mogul. Ductile-iron piston rings will wear in nicely and last a long time.

We suggest using hypereutectic pistons for applications where you expect to run the engine hard, but won't be using nitrous or a supercharger. Hypereutectic pistons are great because of their expansion rate and their durability. Hypereutectics are basically cast pistons, with a high percentage of silicon in the aluminum mix. The result is a stronger piston that won't break down under hard use. It also has a higher melting point than a cast piston, which means you can lean on it a little harder. Since the hypereutectic piston is basically a cast piece, it doesn't expand as much as a forged piston, which means quieter operation when the engine is cold.

Forged pistons are champs when it comes to durability. You can hammer them hard without fear of failure. If you're going to supercharge or blow nitrous into your small-block, forged pistons are the best choice. The downside to forged pistons is noise during cold operation. We have to go with greater piston-to-cylinder-wall clearances with forged pistons because they expand more with heat. This means a rattle when the engine is cold. With this in mind, you need to take it easy on a cold engine in the interest of longer engine life.

Piston selection for the 221-, 260-, 289-, and 302-ci engines is extensive. Various piston types were employed originally to determine compression ratio and performance. Ford dished the pistons found in most 221, 260, 289, and 302 engines to achieve the stock 9.0:1 compression. Higher-compression small-blocks, like the 289-4V and High Performance engines, were fitted with flat-top pistons with valve reliefs. This tells us all small-block Fords from the 1960s had the same size combustion chambers. Ford's original selection of replacement pistons demonstrates the limits of the small-block. The largest oversize piston available from Ford is 4.040 inches. Oversizes up to .060-inch are available from the aftermarket, but again, we discourage a .060-inch overbore.

The standard 289/302 cast piston is a dished unit with valve reliefs. The 289-4V, 302-4V, and 289 High Performance piston was a cast flat-top unit with valve reliefs. Boss 302 engines were fitted with the "D0ZZ-A" or "D0ZZ-B" piston, a TRW forged piece designed for high revs. The Boss piston is different in that it is designed for the Boss 302's canted-valve Cleveland heads. Only one oversize piston was available from the factory for the Boss 302 engine – the "D0ZZ-C" .003-inch oversize forged unit. This was a replacement piston for the piston failure problem that originally plagued the Boss 302.

Piston selection for today's enthusiast lies not at the Ford parts counter, but in the aftermarket. Federal-Mogul (TRW) offers the enthusiast a wealth of stock and aftermarket performance replacement pistons ranging from standard to .060-

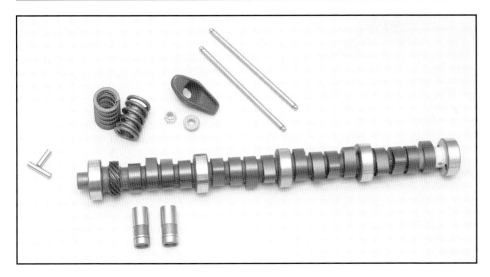

Small-block Fords built prior to 1985 were equipped with flat-tappet camshafts. For budget rebuilds for street engines, a flat-tappet camshaft will get the job done effectively. The downside to flat-tappet cams is the efficiency lost from the friction involved and dated cam lobe technology. Aggressive flat-tappet camshafts aren't as forgiving as their roller-tappet cousins when it comes to idle quality.

inch oversize, from stock compression to high compression, plus cast, hypereutectic, and forged derivatives.

FLYWHEELS AND FLEXPLATES

There's a huge variety of flywheels and flexplates that fit the small-block Ford. Careful selection is important here because issues, such as balance and proper fit, are critical. Choose the incorrect flywheel and you may have problems with starter engagement or find yourself with a balance problem. All Ford small-blocks are externally balanced. All 221-, 260-, 289-, and 302-ci engines built prior to 1982 have a 28-ounce counterweight in the flywheel and harmonic balancer. Beginning in 1982, the 5.0L engine's counter-weighting was revised to 50 ounces. Keep this in mind whenever you're shopping for a harmonic balancer or flywheel.

The main thing to recognize when you're shopping for a flywheel or flex-plate is fitment and offset balance. Do you have a 164-tooth flywheel or do you have a 157-tooth? The 164-tooth flywheel mandates the larger bellhousing, and this is easily discovered because the 164-tooth flywheel won't fit inside the 157-tooth bellhousing. The late-model, 50-ounce flywheel/flexplate is a 157-tooth unit. It will fit in the larger 164-tooth bellhousing, so make sure you don't get them confused.

HARMONIC BALANCERS

As with flywheels, choosing the correct harmonic balancer is critical. Balancer selection is quite simple, however; it just depends on engine and application. The 221 and 260 use a C4OE-6316-A balancer, which is different from the C4AE-6316-C or D balancer common to the 289. Both of these balancers are approximately 1 inch in width and 6-3/8 inches in diameter.

The 289 High Performance balancer is 3-37/64 inches wide. It's heavier because it has to compensate for the heavier Hi-Po connecting rods. It's a similar story for the Boss 302 engine, which employs a wider balancer than its 302 counterpart.

It's important to remember the significance of three-bolt and four-bolt harmonic balancers. From 1962 to '69, all small-block Fords, including the Boss 302, had three-bolt harmonic balancers. This is important when you are planning your engine's front dress. Few things are more discouraging than being on the home stretch of an engine installation, ready to fire it up, and discovering that your three-bolt crankshaft pulley won't bolt onto the four-bolt balancer.

From 1970 on up, all small-block Fords, including the Boss 302 and 351 Cleveland (351M and 400M too!) have a four-bolt harmonic balancer. When the small-block Ford became fuel-injected in the 1980s, the harmonic balancer gained a magnetic trigger and took on a new shape, so it's easy to identify.

OILING SYSTEM

When we get beyond the whirling, pulsing internals of a small-block Ford, we need to look at the support systems that keep it all going. Let's start with the oil sump, pump, and oiling system. Engines built for street use need little more than a high-volume oil pump and some oiling system modifications that improve flow. The oil pump needs to have its rotor side clearances properly checked before installation. While you are in there, it's time well spent to check the pressure relief valve for freedom of movement and proper operation. Check all of the passages to ensure they are clear. Sometimes, rough castings make it through production with blocked passages.

We suggest installing a heavy-duty oil pump driveshaft, even in a stock application. Even though the stock oil pump shaft does a pretty good job, it is added security to go with a heavy-duty shaft just to keep things safe.

Regardless of how clean your original oil pan pick-up is, let's start off right with a new pick-up. This prevents any chance of debris getting into the oil pump and oiling system. We'll get into oiling system modifications in Chapter 4.

When it comes to stock oil pans, pumps, and pick-ups, you have some options. You can go with a Boss 302 oil pan, which offers protection against windage down under. Because this pan is baffled, it keeps the oil around the pick-up in hard cornering.

Camshaft Terms and Tech

WORKBENCH TIP

What makes one camshaft different from another? It is called profile. Profile is lobe design, dimension, and positioning, which controls when it opens the valves, when it closes the valves, how long it keeps the valves open, and how far the valves open. All of these factors play into how the engine will perform.

Flat-tappet camshafts work differently from roller-tappet camshafts, which means we have to think differently with each type. Flat-tappet camshafts limit what we can do with lobe profile if we want good drivability. If we want an aggressive profile with flat tappets, we can only go so far with a street engine or suffer with poor drivability (rough idle, low manifold vacuum). If you want an aggressive profile in a street engine, we suggest stepping up to a roller camshaft, which can handle the aggressive profile better using roller tappets.

- **Lift** is the maximum amount a valve-lifter-pushrod combo can be raised off the base circle. Lift is measured in thousandths of an inch (.000"). Lobe profile determines whether the lift comes on smoothly or abruptly.

- **Duration** is the amount of time the valve is open (measured in degrees), beginning when the valve unseats. Duration typically begins at .004 inch of cam lift or when the lifter begins to ride the ramp coming off the base circle. "Duration at Fifty" means that duration begins at .050 inch of cam lift. Duration at .050 is the industry standard for determining camshaft lobe duration. When you're reading camshaft specs, this is the spec you will see.

- **Lobe Separation** (also known as lobe centerline) is the distance (in degrees) between the intake lobe peak and the exhaust lobe peak. Lobe separation generally runs between 102 and 114 degrees (camshaft degrees).

- **Intake Centerline** is the position of the camshaft in relation to the crankshaft. For example, an intake centerline of 114 degrees means the intake valve reaches maximum lift at 114 degrees after top dead center (ATDC).

- **Exhaust Centerline** is basically the same thing as intake centerline. It is when the exhaust valve reaches maximum lift in degrees before top dead center (BTDC).

- **Valve Overlap** is the period of time when both the intake and exhaust valve are both open to allow for proper cylinder scavenging. Overlap occurs when the exhaust valve is closing and the piston is reaching top dead center. The intake charge from the opening intake valve pushes the exhaust gasses out. Valve overlap is also known as lobe separation. Camshaft grinders can change lobe separation or "valve overlap" to modify the performance of a camshaft. Sometimes they do this rather than change lift or duration.

- **Ramp** is the ascending or descending side of the cam lobe coming off the base circle when lift begins to occur.

- **Flank** is the ascending or descending portion of the lobe past the base circle nearest maximum lift.

- **Heel** is the bottom-most portion of the camshaft's lobe.

- **Base Circle** is the portion of the lobe that doesn't generate lift.

- **Adjustable Valve Timing** is being able to dial in a camshaft by adjusting valve timing at the timing sprocket. By adjusting the valve timing at the sprocket, we can increase or decrease torque. Advance valve timing and you increase torque. Retard valve timing and you lose torque.

Because Boss 302 oil pans tend to be elusive, the aftermarket offers more options for less money. Canton Racing Products offers a Boss 302-style oil pan (#15-600 for 289/302 or #15-650 for 351W) with the same kind of anti-slosh baffling. There is also a high-capacity, seven-quart "T" pan for street and road-racing applications (#15-610 for 289/302 or #15-660 for 351W), which offers greater capacity and baffling for cornering. It keeps oil around the pick-up under all conditions.

A good high-volume oil pump is what you want for street and weekend racing applications. Good oiling is certainly about pressure, but it is more about volume – plenty of oil at all times to moving parts. Pressure becomes important when revs increase. Figure on 10 psi for every 1,000 rpm. At 5,000 rpm, you're going to need 50 psi. But, you don't want 50 psi at idle. Ideally, you will have 20 to 25 psi at idle.

Roller camshafts, though more expensive, yield huge benefits in performance. They yield better performance for two reasons – less friction and more aggressive cam profiles. A more radical roller cam profile allows for a more aggressive ramp up during valve opening without hurting idle quality. During roller cam installation, engine assembly lube is all you have to use on the lobes, roller tappets, and journals. Molybdenum grease is what we use on flat-tappet cam lobes – never on roller cam lobes.

Fox-body Fords call for a different type of double-sump oil pan designed for this platform. Canton offers two basic types of oil pans for Fox-body cars – a drag racing pan and a road-race pan. The #15-620 for the 302 yields a deep sump for the demands of drag racing. So does the #15-670 pan for 351W in these applications. This deep sump pan holds seven quarts and ensures a steady supply of oil around the pick-up under hard acceleration. There are actually three different front sump depth-versions of this pan. See Canton for more details.

When you're going road racing or expect to see a lot of canyon chasing, the Canton #15-640 (302) or #15-670 (351W) is what you want. This is a baffled seven-quart, road-racing pan designed to keep oil around the pick-up in all kinds of cornering.

CAMSHAFTS

The camshaft and valvetrain directly determine not only an engine's personality, but also how reliably an engine will perform throughout its service life. When it comes to camshafts, there are probably more misconceptions than there are facts. We're here to dissolve most of the myths and get you headed in the right direction on your small-block project.

To understand how to pick a camshaft and valvetrain, we must first understand how it all works. Choosing a camshaft profile is rooted in how we want an engine to perform. Are we building a street engine where low- and mid-range torque are important, or are we building a high-revving racing engine that makes peak torque in the high revs?

A camshaft manufacturer's catalog lists dozens of camshaft types for the same type of engine. This is where it gets mighty confusing for the first-time engine builder. We see words like lift, duration, lobe separation, base circle, lobe centerline angle, and valve overlap. What does this information mean and how will it affect your engine's performance?

One rule we tend to forget about in engine building is you can go with a stock camshaft grind, which all of the aftermarket manufacturers have avail-

Besides a roller camshaft and lifters, you can also add roller rockers. Roller rockers will tolerate a more aggressive camshaft, and they also reduce friction, which will boost power.

engines, not to mention the GT-40 1993-95 5.0L Cobra V-8. The nice thing about all of it is packaging. Comp Cams and Crane, for example, offer complete camshaft and valvetrain kits that include compatible springs and cam profiles. All you have to do is order the kit and do the installation. A kit provides a no-brainer solution that ensures you'll have components that work well together.

There seems to be a greater variety of roller-tappet camshafts available out there that allow you to dial in performance. The nice thing about roller cams is the aggressiveness they offer without sacrificing idle quality and drivability. Roller cams are better because they greatly reduce internal friction and allow for more aggressive ramp speeds and lifts, without sacrificing drivability. The roller cam is clearly a better choice for these reasons.

Let's talk more about cam selection and choices. In the old days, we had two basic choices – mechanical and hydraulic flat-tappet camshafts. We went with mechanical camshafts whenever we were going to spin the engine at high RPM. A mechanical cam gave us the precision needed for high-RPM operation, because mechanical lifters don't pump up at high revs. We adjust the valve lash and watch what the engine does at high RPM. Mechanical lifters are nothing more than the middle

able. You can go with a dead stock camshaft, get a smooth idle and good low-end torque. Crane, for example, has a flat-tappet 289 High Performance grind available that will give your 289/302 build that genuine Hi-Po sound. There are mild and aggressive grinds available for 5.0L High Output

A popular misconception is that flat tappets ride squarely on the cam lobe. Flat-tappet lifters ride on the cam lobe offset like this. They spin on the lobe for less friction and uniform wear.

Budget builds call for a regular timing set like this one. Contrary to popular shop talk, this is a good timing set for mild street engines because there is less chain stretch than we see with dual-roller timing sets. The up side to dual roller timing sets is less friction.

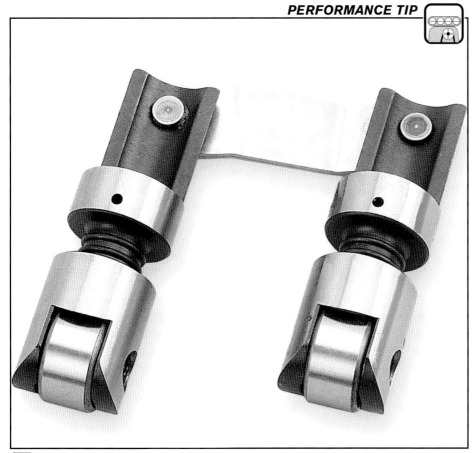

Roller lifters joined together like these from Lunati work together without the need for a spider and dog bones like we find with most roller-cam kits. The penalty here is cost – these are more expensive than the spider/dog-bone roller tappets.

man between the cam lobe and valve.

Hydraulic lifters were conceived to take maintenance out of the equation because they automatically adjust themselves. The hydraulic lifter's internal piston rides on a cushion of oil pressure that keeps everything snug against the pushrod, rocker arm, and valvestem. As the cam lobes and other valvetrain parts wear, the lifter takes up the slack, keeping the entire valvetrain nice and snug. Hydraulic lifters tend to "pump up" at high revs, making them undesirable for extreme racing applications.

Roller tappets are nothing new, even when they were introduced in Ford factory production engines in 1985. They reduce internal friction and give the valvetrain greater levels of precision. Roller tappets also allow us to run more aggressive cam lobe profiles that give us more power without adversely affecting drivability. Like flat tappets, roller tap-

pets are available both in mechanical (solid) and hydraulic.

CAMSHAFTS – THE INSIDE DOPE

Always bear in mind what you're going to have for induction, heads, and exhaust. The sharp engine builder understands that in order to work effectively, an engine must have matched components. Cam, valvetrain, heads, intake manifold, and an exhaust system must all work as a team or you're just wasting time and money. If you're going to use stock heads, which we expect with a stock or near-stock engine, your cam profile need not be too aggressive. Opt for a cam profile that will give you good low- and mid-range torque. Power doesn't do you much good on the street when it happens at 6,500 rpm.

The best street performance cams are ground with a lobe separation

between 108 and 114 degrees. When we keep lobe separation above 112 degrees, we improve drivability because the engine idles smoother and makes better low-end torque. This is what we want from a street engine. Anytime lobe separation is below 108 degrees, idle quality and streetability suffer. But there's more to it than just lobe separation.

Compression and cam timing must be considered together because one always affects the other. Valve timing events directly affect cylinder pressure. Long intake valve duration reduces cylinder pressure. Shorter duration increases cylinder pressure. Too much cylinder pressure can cause detonation (pinging), but have too little and you lose torque. You can count on cam manufacturers to figure stock compression ratios into their camshaft selection tables, which makes choosing a camshaft easier than it's ever been. Search manufacturers' websites for their recommendations based on your application and you will be pleased with the result most of the time.

The greatest advice we can offer the beginner is to be conservative with your cam specs if you want reliability and long life. Keep with a conservative lift profile with under .500 inch of lift. High-lift camshafts beat the daylights out of a valvetrain, and they put valve-to-piston clearances at risk. Instead of opening the valve farther (lift), we want to open it longer (duration) and in better efficiency with piston timing (overlap or lobe separation).

Valve overlap is the period between exhaust stroke and intake stroke where both valves are slightly open. This improves exhaust scavenging by allowing the incoming intake charge to push remaining exhaust gasses out via the closing exhaust valve. Were the exhaust valve completely closed, we wouldn't get any scavenging. The greater the overlap in a street engine, the less torque the engine will make down low where we need it most. This is why we want less valve overlap in a street engine and more in a racing engine, which will make its torque at high RPM. Street engines need 10 to 55 degrees of valve overlap to make good torque. When valve overlap starts getting above 55 degrees, torque on the low end begins to go away. A really hot street engine might need more than 55 degrees of valve overlap, but not much more. To give you an idea of what we're talking about, racing engines need 70 to 115 degrees of valve overlap. For a street engine, we want valve overlap to maximize torque, which means taking a conservative approach.

You should also consider lobe separation angle when choosing your cam. Choose a lobe separation angle based on displacement, valve sizing, and how the engine will be used. The smaller the valves, the tighter (fewer degrees) lobe separation should be. However, tighter lobe separation does adversely affect idle quality. This is why most camshaft manufacturers spec their cams with wider lobe separations than the custom grinders.

Duration is likely the most important dynamic to consider for a street engine. We can increase duration whenever we want to run less lift. Why? Because we get airflow into the cylinder bore two ways – lift and duration. We can open the valve farther (more lift) for less time (duration), or we can open the valve less and keep it open longer to get the same amount of airflow. Each way will have a different effect on performance. Excessive duration hurts low-end torque, which is what we need on the street, so we have to achieve a balance between lift and duration.

Valve lift is an issue we must think about as it pertains to an engine's needs. Small-blocks generally need more valve lift than big-blocks. As we increase lift, generally we increase torque. This is especially important at low- and mid-rpm ranges where it counts on the street. Low-end torque is harder to achieve with a small-block because these engines generally sport short strokes and large bores. Your objective needs to be more torque with less RPM if you want your engine to live longer. High revs are what drain the life out of an engine quickly.

So, to make good low-end torque with a small-block, we need a camshaft that will offer a combination of effective lift and duration. As a rule, we want to run a longer intake duration to make the most of valve lift.

ROCKER ARMS

We get valve lift via the camshaft, to be sure. But, rocker-arm ratio is the other half of the equation. The most common rocker-arm ratio is 1.6:1, which means the rocker arm will give the valve 1.6 times the lift we have at the cam lobe. When we step up to a 1.7:1 ratio rocker arm, valve lift becomes 1.7 times that which we find at the lobe.

When we're planning a valvetrain, it is best to achieve a good balance. If you run a high-lift camshaft with a 1.7:1 rocker-arm ratio, you may be getting too much lift, which means excessive wear and tear. It is best to err on the conservative side, especially if you're building an engine for daily use. Whenever you opt for an aggressive camshaft with a lot of lift, you're putting more stress on the valvestem, guide, and spring. Hammering the valvetrain daily with excessive lift can kill an engine without warning.

We will take this excessive wear logic a step further. It is vital that you ascertain proper centering of the rocker-arm tip on the valvestem tip when you're setting up the valvetrain. We do this by using the correct length pushrod for the application. Buy a pushrod checker at your favorite speed shop if ever you're in doubt. A pushrod checker is little more than an adjustable pushrod that you can use to determine rocker arm geometry. If the pushrod is too long, the tip will be under-centered on the valvestem, causing excessive side loads toward the outside of the cylinder head. If the pushrod is too short, the rocker-arm tip will be over-centered, causing excessive side loading toward the inside of the head. In either case, side loads on the valvestem and guide cause excessive wear and early failure. This is why we want the rocker-arm tip to be properly centered on the valvestem for smooth operation.

One accessory that will reduce valvestem tip wear and side loading is the roller-tip rocker arm. Roller-tip rocker arms roll smoothly across the valvestem tip, virtually eliminating wear. Stamped steel, roller tip rocker-arms are available at budget prices without the high cost of extruded or forged pieces.

WATER PUMPS

Timing covers and water pumps have evolved side by side since 1962. Small-block Fords had cast-aluminum water pumps from 1962 to '65. Beginning in 1965, 289 High Performance engines were equipped with cast-iron water pumps. From 1966 through the early 1980s, all small-block Fords were equipped with cast-iron water pumps from the factory. All water pumps prior to 1970 have the inlet on the right-hand side. From 1970 and up, the inlet was on the left-hand side. In 1994, Ford redesigned both the timing cover and water pump. The water pump became much smaller and used a reverse-flow design for improved cooling. This water pump can be used only with the serpentine belt drive.

Water pump selection is pretty simple. Even in a stock small-block Ford, you want a high-flow water pump. Because most small-block Fords live in tight, cramped engine compartments with limited airflow, coolant needs to move aggressively through the radiator and engine to maximize cooling system performance.

Weiand and Edelbrock offer the enthusiast a variety of high-flow water pumps for small-block Fords, including the Cleveland. Using these pumps is a no-brainer. Auto parts stores like Auto-Zone and Advanced Auto Parts offer stock replacement water pumps as well as high-flow types. Shop carefully and make the most of your water pump purchase.

COOLING FANS AND RADIATORS

It's impossible to think about water pumps without thinking of the cooling fan. There are all kinds of opinions about engine cooling fans. One basic opinion holds true throughout. Fans should be efficient, meaning they move air only when they need to put as little drag on the engine as possible. The humble thermostatic clutch fan is the most efficient engine-driven fan going, since it only runs when the engine is hot. After that, the flex-blade fan creates less drag with engine speed, but it runs all the time since it has no clutch. Electric cooling fans make the most sense from an effi-

Timing Covers

The small-block Ford has been equipped with three basic types of timing covers throughout its production life. From 1962 to '67, the timing pointer was cast into the cover. Beginning in 1968, Ford went to a bolt-on timing pointer and a wider three-bolt harmonic balancer. This timing cover continued through the early 1980s. When the 5.0L CFI and SEFI small-blocks debuted during the 1980s, the timing pointer was moved to the right-hand side of the timing cover. Beginning in 1994, Ford went to a redesigned timing cover and a smaller reverse-flow water pump.

Most replacement timing covers have this provision for a front dipstick tube with front-sump oil pans. If you are building a vintage small-block with the front sump, this provision needs to be drilled out before installation. Late-model, dual-sump pans don't need this provision drilled out.

IMPORTANT STEP

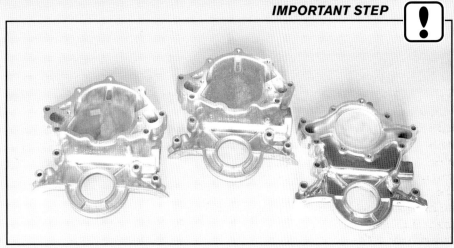

Since 1962, Ford has produced a variety of timing covers for the small-block Ford. Here are three basic types. From left, 1962 to '67 with the cast-in timing pointer, 1968 to '85 with the bolt-on timing pointer, and the 1994 to present timing cover for the reverse-flow water pump. There are variations in these covers, especially from 1968 up.

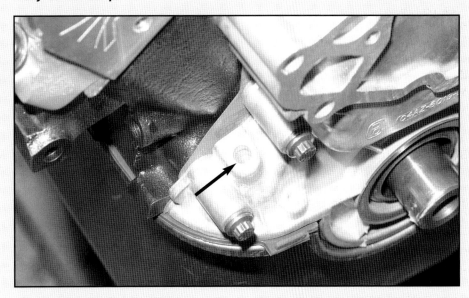

ciency standpoint because they come on only as needed and put the least drag on the engine. Electric fans tend to be more involved to install and use, which can be a drawback. Whatever type of fan you choose, use a fan shroud to pull and direct air through the radiator.

Stock to mild performance builds will live happily with a water pump-driven fan. A flex-fan from Flex-A-Lite runs qui-etly and consumes less power than a stock steel fan, especially the four-, six-, and seven-blade types. If your Ford has the stock flex-fan used in the late 1960s into the 1970s – replace it immediately. These fans have a reputation for blade failure.

The most efficient fan out there is the humble luxury car thermostatic clutch fan, which is quiet and consumes power only when needed. Make sure you opt for a thermostatic clutch fan, and not just a clutch fan. Clutch fans run all the time. Thermostatic clutch fans engage only as needed. Make sure you use a fan shroud to increase airflow velocity through the radiator. Plus, make sure half of the fan is in the shroud and half is out for best results.

Most vintage Fords were equipped with woefully inadequate two-row core radiators from the factory. This

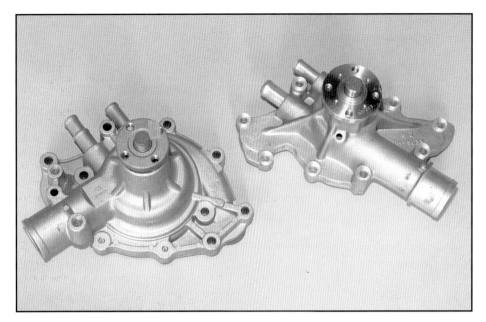

Here's a Weiand High-Flow water pump for 1970 and up small-block Fords. Note the left-hand inlet.

Water pumps, like timing covers, have evolved since 1962. From 1962 to '65, small-block Fords had aluminum water pumps. From 1966 through the early 1980s, Ford used a cast-iron water pump. With the advent of 5.0L performance in the 1980s came a redesigned water pump. Another difference is right-hand versus left-hand inlet water pumps. From 1962 to '69, small-block Fords had a right-hand inlet. From 1970 on up, they had a left-hand inlet. Shown here are two examples. On the left is a 1962 to '69 replacement water pump in cast aluminum. On the right is a 1994 and up reverse-flow water pump.

shortcoming improved during the 1980s. Nonetheless, a stock radiator for the 289 or the 392-inch stroker in your '65 Mustang isn't going to be enough. The stock 289 or 302 has a tough enough time. Toss the stroker into this equation and you have a formula for overheating.

The cross-flow radiator is the most efficient radiator going because it offers a broader cooling surface area. Aluminum radiators make the best heat sinks for hot engines. Although there is a lot of debate over aluminum versus brass radiators, aluminum radiators get the nod more and more these days from racers and automakers alike. They are lighter, and they cool considerably better than their copper and brass counterparts.

CARBURETORS

The induction system can yield the single greatest gains in power if you use the right parts. Contrary to what you've been taught through the years, bigger isn't always better when it comes to carburetors and throttle bodies. A good rule of thumb is that small-blocks up to 351 ci need no more than 650 cfm unless you're running a really radical camshaft and heads at high RPM. Even small-blocks stroked to 400 ci need 550 to 650 cfm. When displacement rises to 400 to 450 ci, carburetor sizing should increase to 700 to 750 cfm. Here's a quick-reference chart below.

Carburetor type and sizing boils down to how you will drive the vehicle. Street engines do well with a variety of carburetor types. Holley's tried and proven 4150/4160 series carburetors have been in steady use for nearly five decades. They're basically the same design as they were in the 1960s. However, Holley has made some significant

improvements in its carburetors in recent times. It's now easier to tune them because there is a wealth of information available from Holley to keep them in proper tune. The downside to the Holley 4150 and 4160 is losing fuel all over the intake manifold when it is time to do jet and power valve swaps.

Edelbrock and Carter make similar carburetors (based on the Carter AFB and AVS design) that are as time-proven as the Holley. What gives the Edelbrock and Carter carbs the edge is reliability and serviceability. Pop the top off these carburetors for easy jet, needle, and spring swaps, and then go take a test drive. You can access the carburetor's internals without spilling fuel all over the intake manifold. Look for one in the right size for your engine.

Ford's factory 4100 series four-barrel carburetor, available in 480 to 600 cfm sizes, is the undisputed champ for reliability and serviceability. It was used on small-block Fords from 1963 until '66. In 1967, the 4100 was replaced with the emissions-friendly Autolite 4300, which is not a suggested carburetor. The 4100 uses Holley parts, like the power valve and jetting. Yet, it requires less maintenance and upkeep

Engine Displacement	Recommended Street Carburetor Sizing	Recommended Racing Carburetor Sizing
221-260 ci	400-500 cfm	500-600 cfm
289-302 ci	480-600 cfm	600-650 cfm
351-400 ci	550-650 cfm	600-750 cfm
400-500 ci	600-700 cfm	650-850 cfm

than the Holley. You can tune a 4100 just like you tune the Holley 4150/4160. Despite the harshness of today's gasoline, the 4100 is a stable, reliable performer. For mild to aggressive small-blocks and even mild big-blocks, the 4100 is an outstanding carburetor. Install it, set it, forget it – that's the Autolite 4100.

Multiple carburetor setups, like 6- and 8-bbls, are terrific for occasional drivers and impressing the masses at cruising spots. But multiple carburetion has little advantage for the daily driver. An engine needs to have a radical attitude before multiple carburetion is of any benefit. By radical, we mean aggressive camming and heads. Mild street engines won't benefit from multiple carburetion because they won't manage airflow successfully. Generally, engines that are over-carbed stumble on the excessive air/fuel flow, foul spark plugs, and lose precious life because oil gets washed off the cylinder walls. If you want multi-carburetion for its looks, there's nothing better for visual stimulation. With tri-power setups, you can shut fuel off to the secondary carburetors and enjoy 2V carburetion. The same can be said for the secondary carburetor on an 8V induction package.

INTAKE MANIFOLDS

If you aren't stuck on the idea of using a stock intake manifold, you can pick up an aluminum manifold from the aftermarket that will probably offer you better performance. For carbureted street engines, use a good dual-plane aluminum intake manifold like the Edelbrock Performer or Weiand Stealth. These manifolds offer excellent low-end torque while yielding good high-end response and breathing to 6,000 rpm. They're able to do all this by employing long intake runners that are also large enough for high-RPM use. Long runners give us velocity and volume, which results in excellent low- to mid-range torque. Runner height and volume feeds the engine on the high end.

A single-plane manifold like the Edelbrock Victor Jr. doesn't perform as well on the street because it's designed for high-RPM use only. It helps the engine gulp huge quantities of air at

high RPM. A single-plane manifold doesn't afford our engine the air velocity and appropriate volume it needs at low revs. By "single-plane," we mean there's no crossover or the double-decker design, as with dual-plane manifolds. With a single-plane manifold, air and fuel gather at the plenum and go straight into the intake ports. This is what an engine needs at high RPM.

You can save money by searching the swap meets for a good used intake manifold. A used manifold can be media blasted to look like new, and no one will know it's used but you. Manifolds to watch for are the older Edelbrock dual-planes manifolds like the F4B, Streetmaster, and Cobra high-risers. Older manifolds offer outstanding performance without the "new" price tag. Rare and collectible Cobra high-rise manifolds can cost more than a new aftermarket manifold. So watch out for high prices there. Reproduction Cobra high-rise manifolds are available from Tony D. Branda Mustang & Shelby. These are great if you want a period look, without having to shop around for weeks.

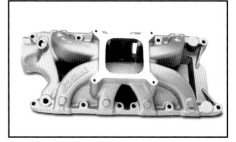

The Edelbrock Performer RPM intake manifold gives us the best of both worlds in street performance. Because it's a dual-plane intake manifold, it has longer intake runners, which help the engine make better low- and mid-range torque. Since these long runners have high ceilings, they help the engine make torque at high revs.

IGNITION

There has been plenty of black magic in and around ignition systems over the years. You can gain power with a hot ignition system. Generally, the hotter and longer the spark, the more completely the mixture is burnt. This is especially true with high-compression and

ECONOMY STEP

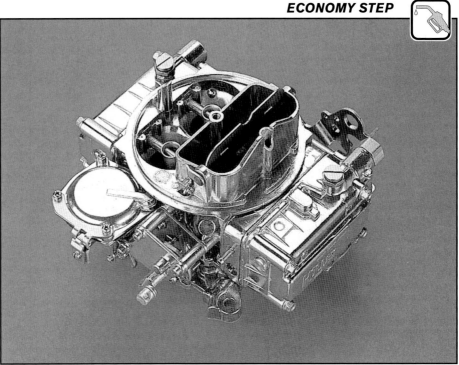

Here's the 4160 Holley 600-cfm carburetor, which is a perfect fit for the small-block Ford. This is a logical replacement for the Autolite 4100 if you can't find a good one. Any of the Holley 4150/4160 carburetors works well on the small block Ford. Just get your sizing and jetting right in the process.

$ *If you're on a tight budget, the Ignitor from Pertronix is an excellent, affordable way to get into electronic ignition in a stock Autolite/Motorcraft distributor. This little fellow is big on performance and installs in 15 minutes.*

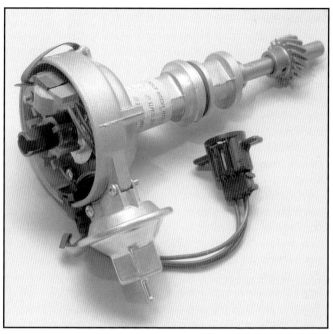

Ford's Duraspark ignition fits right into a small-block Ford and has an external ignition amplifier you can mount just about anywhere.

This is the Ignitor II from Pertronix. Unlike the standard Ignitor, the Ignitor II changes the dwell angle as revs increase.

minutes to install. The bad things about the Ignitor are the Autolite and Motorcraft distributors it is designed for! These distributors employ two bushings that suffer from inadequate lubrication, so they wear out quickly. The Ignitor makes huge allowances for distributor shaft side play, where points won't.

MSD, Mallory, Accel, and Jacobs Electronics all offer the enthusiast high-quality aftermarket ignition systems ranging from distributors to ignition coils and exciter packages. The result is improved performance when you mash the throttle. But always keep in mind that you're not going to see the huge performance gains from an ignition upgrade on a stock engine. A hotter, longer spark improves emissions, idle quality, fuel economy, and low-end torque. Any way you slice or dice it, ignition improvements enhance drivability and reliability. They're worth every penny.

Power management boils down to making the right decisions during the planning stages of your engine build, which is covered in Chapter 1. Planning for power involves consulting the right people and ultimately using the right parts when it's time to get to work.

Choosing the right distributor depends on how you intend to use the

supercharged engines that tend to snuff out a mild-mannered spark.

However, tight budgets and mild applications demand simple solutions. The Pertronix Ignitor ignition retrofit is the easiest ignition upgrade there is. Pop the distributor cap, remove the points and condenser, and install the Ignitor. Because we have seen this innovative retrofit dozens of times, we know it works. The Ignitor improves idle quality and throttle response, and it takes 15

engine. All street-driven engines need a vacuum advance distributor. This provides a nice, seamless transition from idle power to acceleration, advancing the spark as needed under acceleration. The vacuum advance provides good initial spark advance before handing this job off to the centrifugal advance. This is important to remember regardless of the brand name. MSD, Accel, and Mallory all have vacuum advance distributors for mild performance applications. When you choose a distributor, always opt on the side of reliability and tune ability. You want a distributor you can tune for your application and expected use. This means something you can drive to work with, then tune for the drag strip or road racecourse on the weekends. Although some point-triggered ignitions are still available, always go with electronic ignition for best results.

Distributors without vacuum advance units are more for racing applications where the engine is going to be revving higher as it gets underway. Mechanical advance distributors don't make sense for the street because they don't give us the seamless spark advance needed for street use.

Spark enhancers make more sense for racing than they do for street use. It

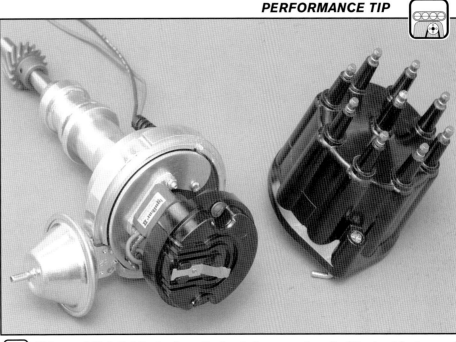

This new billet distributor from Pertronix incorporates all of the best features of the distributors we are familiar with and rolls them into one. It has the Ignitor II module for outstanding performance. The rotor is the same kind we find in vintage Delco distributors, which means you can find it anywhere. The cap is easy to remove and install, and is available in male and female terminal designs.

is good to have a hotter spark in any situation because it does improve both efficiency and emissions. If you're going to spin your engine high or be using a power adder like nitrous oxide or super-charging, spark enhancers become a mandatory accessory. The last thing you need under the gun of nitrous is a misfire or pre-ignition, which can do major engine damage.

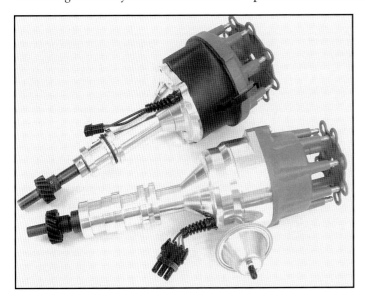

MSD Ignition needs no introduction with performance buffs because this is the most oft-used ignition system in racing. For racing applications, we really don't need a vacuum advance. For street applications, the vacuum advance helps us get started. MSD has a distributor for just about every application.

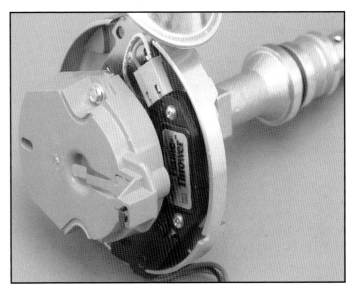

Pertronix introduces this HEI distributor for small-block Fords. What makes this distributor a best buy is the ignition coil that's housed in the distributor cap. This means not having to find a place for the coil.

CHAPTER 4

MACHINE SHOP

When you arrive at the machine shop with your engine, there are going to be all kinds of questions from the machinist that you'll have to answer. The machinists will want to know what you want done to the engine. This chapter should help you figure that out ahead of time. First, you need to have all castings and components thoroughly cleaned, which is normally performed by the machine shop.

Once these parts are completely cleaned, it's time for machine work.

So what is all this machine work about? Why is it necessary, and what can we do without when we're on a budget? First, we have to understand the difference between an engine "overhaul" and a "rebuild." An engine overhaul is little more than a ring and bearing job, which costs less and buys the owner some time. Think of an engine overhaul as a band-

aid fix. The band-aid keeps you from bleeding excessively, but it doesn't heal the cut. It only buys you time.

When we do an engine overhaul, we knock the engine down to the bare block, cut the ridges at the tops of the cylinders (in order to get the pistons and rods out), run a ball hone up and down the cylinders to cut the glaze, inspect the bearings, and replace what needs to be replaced. An overhaul just tightens

---

George's Machine Shop Check List

WORKBENCH TIP

Block Work

A: Bore cylinders to next oversize if tapered more than .011 inch.
B: Hone cylinders to true piston size.
C: Check line bore – hone or bore as necessary.
D: Hone lifter bores.
E: Check block deck for trueness. Mill as necessary.
F: Check all oil galleys. Clean thoroughly with solvent and wire brush.
G: Inspect and clean all water jackets.
H: Chase and repair all threads.

Rotating Assembly Work

A: Inspect crankshaft for trueness (is it straight?) and cracking.
B: Measure crank, machine journals to next undersize.
C: If journals look good and measure well, polish only.
D: Inspect and recondition connecting rods.
E: Install new connecting rod bolts.
F: Inspect and reface flywheel (if equipped).
G: Inspect flexplate for cracking (if equipped).
H: Clean and chase threads.
I: Clean and chase all oil passages.

Cylinder Heads

A: Check mating surfaces, mill only as necessary.
B: Replace valves and valveguides.
C: Install hardened exhaust valve seats.
D: Three-angle valve job.
E: Clean and chase all threads.

---

things back up for a while, but it isn't really a permanent fix.

An engine rebuild molds new life into an old, worn-out engine. If performed properly, and with great attention to detail, an engine rebuild can mean 100,000 to 300,000 miles of new life with proper maintenance and use. All this new life, just from complete machining and installing quality parts.

THE BLOCK

We need to begin the block machining process with a thorough cleaning. In the good old days, we used to dunk those nasty castings in a lye tank to get them clean. In the interest of a cleaner environment, machine shops have had to become familiar with new, more responsible cleaning processes. Jim Grubbs Motorsports, which is building this engine, has the latest cleaning technology available. Grubbs begins by cooking dirty, grimy castings at high temperature. Once that process is complete, castings are placed in a rotisserie where they are blasted with steel shot. When castings emerge from the cleaning equipment, they look like brand new iron castings. This is something that old lye tank could never do even on its best day. Not only do we have clearer castings, but we also have a cleaner environment.

With a clean block, we need to check all water jackets and oil passages for cleanliness. Even though our block may look hospital clean, there are areas we are bound to miss if we don't pay close attention. Oil passages and water jackets need a thorough pass with solvent and a wire rat-tail brush. All freeze plugs and oil galley plugs must be removed for this process.

Before we even consider boring the block, we need to check each cylinder bore for taper and other irregularities. We suggest this because some blocks are bored that don't need to be bored. This is wasteful. If cylinder bore taper is less than .011-inch from top to bottom, you can get away with honing, and a fresh set of standard pistons and rings.

Most blocks need to be bored at least .020-inch oversize. If you can get

How To Remove A Broken Bolt
 WORKBENCH TIP

You're bound to run into this sooner or later – the stubborn bolt that has broken off into a block or cylinder head. Sometimes corrosion gets the best of a bolt shank. Other times, the bolt's integrity wasn't much to begin with. And sometimes, people just get stupid and cross-thread bolts into holes that won't come out without a lot of sweat. Our 289 block has several oil pan bolts that have broken off into the block. We're going after them now.

A 1/8-inch drill bit is used to carefully drill the hole we need for the bolt extractor (sometimes called an Easy-Out).

First, we work the damaged bolt with a dye grinder, creating a countersink for the drill bit. This gives the drill bit a place to start.

The bolt extractor is gently tapped into the hole. We twist the extractor counterclockwise, and out comes the bolt.

.020-inch oversize pistons, opt for this size rather than the more traditional .030-inch overbore. This buys the block at least one more rebuild.

Another dynamic we need to check at the same time we check bore taper is the line-bore. The line-bore is the main bearing saddles and caps. We need to check the line-bore for proper alignment and dimension. Most of the time, you can get away with honing the line-bore. We hone the line-bore just like we hone cylinders or recondition connecting rods. When we hone the line-bore, we are scoring the main bearing contact surfaces to improve bearing adhesion with the main caps.

A good machinist thinks of every angle when it comes to the main bearing saddles. At Jim Grubbs Motorsports, we learned it's a good idea to remove the main bearing caps and resize them. We do this by milling each cap, countersinking the bolt-holes, and resizing each of the caps. When we mill the main caps, it throws the main saddles off center. This makes it necessary to bore and resize the main saddles. With the main bearing saddles (line-bore) resized, we have a perfect line-bore. If your budget is limited, resizing the line-bore isn't necessary. But if you want to make an engine like new in every respect, resizing the line-bore is an excellent idea.

Rarely does the line-bore need to be bored and honed. Most blocks have a pretty straight line-bore from the factory, and they tend to stay that way for the life of the block. The line-bore is critical because it is where the crankshaft lives. A line-bore that is out of true will cause abnormal bearing wear and premature crankshaft and bearing failure. This is why we want the line-bore nice and straight.

Once the line-bore is within specifications, the block is bored to the next oversize. As a rule, machine shops bore blocks in stages – give or take .005 inch at a time. With a .030-inch overbore, each cylinder is bored .025 inch, and then it is honed the rest of the way to the piston size. Not all pistons are exactly 4.000 inches or 4.030 inches. Each piston is measured and so is each bore. Piston-to-cylinder-wall clearances can vary a

lot from bore to bore. The seasoned machinist understands that each piston needs to be custom-fitted to each cylinder bore. This is why we measure each piston, and then bore and hone each cylinder for a perfect fit. But, we'll tell you this – not all machine shops match-bore cylinders to fit the pistons. Some will check one bore and assume the rest are an identical fit. This just isn't being smart.

Tight piston-to-cylinder-wall clearances can cost you in lost power and give you an engine that runs too hot because of the internal friction. This is an easy mistake to make because not all machinists think about piston growth – and the dynamics of each piston type. Pistons grow with engine heat. Cast and hypereutectic pistons don't expand at the same rate as forged pistons. With forged pistons, we need to allow more room for expansion when we are boring and honing the bores. Cast and hypereutectic pistons don't need as much room to expand.

Jim Grubbs Motorsports hones cylinders to match-fit the pistons. Jim hones one bore at a time, then hones, then checks, then hones, and checks. This kind of close attention to detail is what makes a Grubbs engine money in the bank for what it ultimately saves you.

The decks (where we park the cylinder heads) are the last machining step. Block decks tend to warp from the excessive heat that occurs in this area. This is where we light the fire and exert the great pressures that give us power. Most of the time, the warpage isn't that bad, which means we can get away with not having to mill the decks. A machinist needs to check each deck with a straight edge to determine its integrity. A good rule of thumb is to "shave" the decks, removing just enough iron to get the surface straight. It's a good idea to make a .005-inch cut and see what the deck looks like. Like we said – just enough to get the deck true, without removing too much.

Thread chasing is one important step that gets overlooked all too often. Thread chasing is simply the act of cleaning up all the threads in the block.

This includes cylinder head bolt threads, main bearing bolt threads, you name it. With clean threads, you get an accurate torque reading when it's time to screw the thing together. Dirty, rusty threads on both bolts and blocks cause bolt threads to bind, giving you inaccurate torque readings and potential engine failure.

A can of WD-40 and a thread chaser cleans things up nicely. Before you go any further, we suggest screwing a test bolt into each hole to determine smoothness. Once threads are chased, a bolt should glide right through the threads without resistance. And when it's time to torque these bolts, readings should be accurate, and you should be confident.

When Ford assembled its small-blocks to begin with, they went with press-in oil galley plugs at the front of the block behind the timing set. Most rebuilders go with these oil galley plugs instead of taking a little extra time and using screw-in oil galley plugs. Jim Grubbs taps the oil galley holes and fits them with screw-in plugs.

The water jackets and oil galleys are also very important. All oil galleys need to be cleaned thoroughly to remove all debris and rust. The cleaning process at Jim Grubbs Motorsports is pretty thorough because it yields a fresh iron casting. However, machine work creates its own kind of debris that must also be removed. With all oil galley plugs removed, the oil galleys must be flushed and chased with a rat-tail brush. This removes any unwanted debris that can harm a fresh engine.

When all machine work is finished, the block is washed thoroughly in what looks like an industrial dishwasher. Hot, steamy water blasts the block, removing any stray dirt and debris. During the wash cycle, the machine is stopped so the oil galleys and water jackets can be chased. The result is a hospital-clean block ready for assembly. Grubbs sprays the cylinder walls and bearing contact surfaces with WD-40 to prevent corrosion. Then, the block is mounted on an engine stand and sealed in a plastic bag.

What Now?

What happens when an engine rebuild becomes the layman's worst nightmare? Our 289 block seems to be a sea of broken-off bolt shanks and drain plugs. The bolt shanks were easy to get, thank goodness. The cooling system drain plugs were not. It appears our cooling system drain plugs were cross-threaded at the Cleveland engine plant 40 years ago. Exposure to hot coolant has seized them permanently into the block. What do you do about seized cooling system drain plugs? Jim Grubbs Motorsports came to the rescue, removing them in short order. But, it wasn't easy. Let's watch.

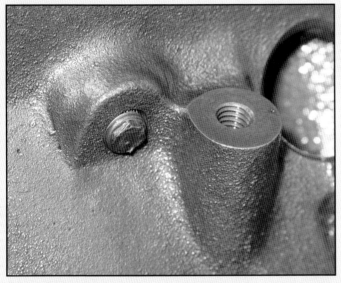

We looked at this one with a sinking feeling in our stomachs. Our very words were – "There's no way..." when it came to getting this drain plug out. Jim Grubbs Motorsports had other ideas.

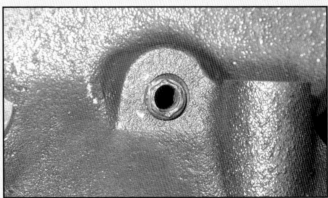

Next, we drill the drain plug through with a 5/16-inch bit.

At first, it looked easy. Just countersink the drain plug and prep it for drilling.

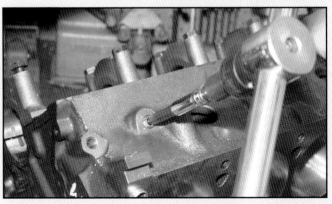

A bolt-extractor is tapped into the drain plug as shown. Next, a good counterclockwise twist. We even heated the block around the drain plug to help expand the iron. You won't believe the result.

What Now? (continued)

WORKBENCH TIP

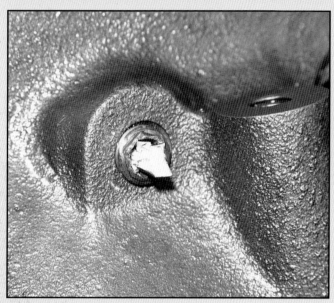

Ouch! All our best efforts couldn't get the drain plug out. We broke the bolt-extractor.

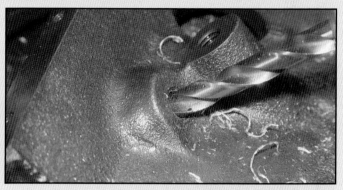

The drain plug had to be removed one agonizing layer at a time using drill bits that were progressively larger with each step.

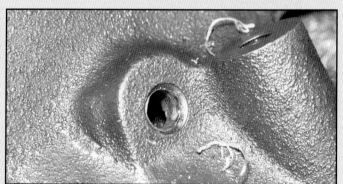

The drain-plug hole has been drilled out as far as it can go at this point. Because it was cross-threaded at the factory, we have threads damaged beyond repair.

Slowly but surely, the super hard bolt-extractor is removed from the drain plug with vice grips. We had to back the bolt-extractor out (clockwise). The drain plug, however, was not budging.

Next, Grubbs runs a tap through the damaged hole and cuts new threads for a new drain plug. The new drain plug will get Teflon tape on the threads to prevent this kind of thing in the future.

Machining the Block

1 Clean the Block

1–Our 289 block is fresh from cleaning, ready for machine work. Jim Grubbs Motorsports has a high-tech cleaning process that is environmentally responsible. Look at the result. It looks like a new old-stock block fresh from its original shipping container.

2 Ready the Block for Line-Boring

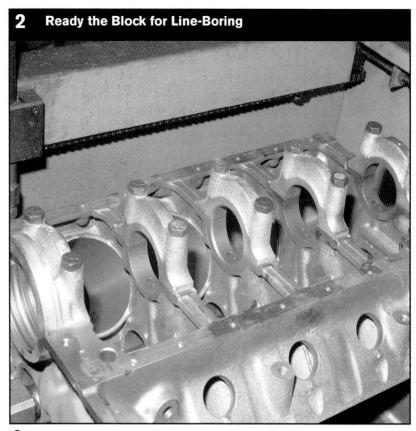

2–Jim Grubbs has positioned the block in the line-boring machine for close inspection and initial machine work.

3 Remove the Main Caps

3–The main caps are removed first to set up the line hone. Once set up, they will be reinstalled and torqued for the honing process.

IMPORTANT STEP !

4 Mill the Main Cap Sides

! *4–Jim Grubbs has decided to resize the line-bore, just to show us how it's done. Each main cap is dressed with a file and milled as shown. Here, we are milling the sides of the thrust main cap. This gets the sides nice and square.*

5   Mill the Main Cap Faces

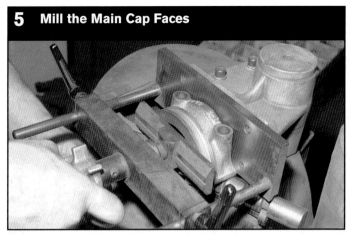

5–Once the sides of each main cap are square, the faces are milled as shown. This gets each main cap square with the block.

IMPORTANT STEP !

7   Countersink the Bolt Holes

! *7–Bolt holes are countersunk for ease of bolt installation and to reduce the risk of stress cracking.*

TORQUING FASTENERS

9   Torque the Cap Bolts

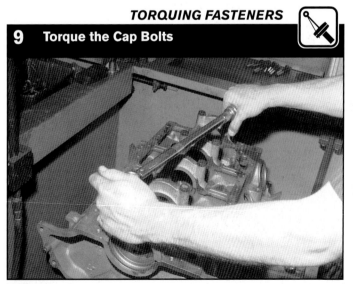

9–Main caps are torqued to 60 to 70 ft-lbs before the line-bore is cut.

6   Remove Rough Edges

6–Each main cap is dressed with a file as shown to remove any rough edges created during the milling process.

8   Lubricate the Cap Bolts

8–Main bearing cap bolts are lubricated with engine oil for smooth, accurate torque readings.

PRECISION MEASUREMENT

10   Check the Main Caps

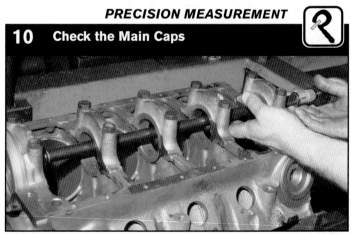

10–Main bearing cap dimensions are checked to get a baseline before machine work begins. With a baseline dimension, the machinist has something to work with as a reference. This tells us how much metal has been removed from each of the main caps during the honing process.

11   Hone the Caps

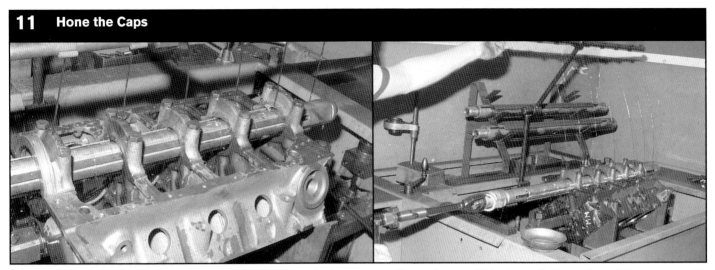

11–With the main caps torqued into place, Grubbs runs the hone across the main caps. This step gets the main saddles square with the main caps. It also puts a crosshatch pattern in the mains, which keeps the bearings more secure. The line-hone is powered by a large drill, which is hand propelled back and forth to cut the mains and caps.

12   Check the Mains

12–The main bearing saddles have a nice crosshatch pattern, which will keep the main bearings secure. And because we have main saddles that are true, there will be no unnecessary stress on the crankshaft.

13–The boring bar is set up to take this block's standard 4.000-inch bores and cut them .025-inch oversize. Boring the block removes the taper and gets the bores true. Three passes are made to bore each cylinder to 4.025 inches.

13   Bore the Block

14 Mill the Decks

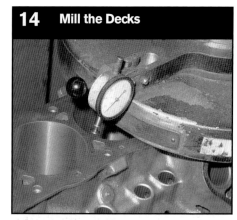

14–Next, the block's decks are milled in small steps to ensure we only remove just enough iron to make the decks true. Whenever we mill the block's decks, we are changing the geometry between the heads and the intake manifold. This is why we need to take it slow and shave only the amount necessary.

15 Inspect the Decks

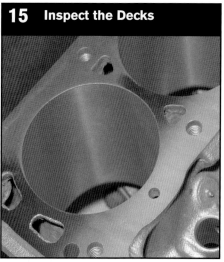

15–One pass with the mill nets this result at the block deck. You can see where this block is warped near the coolant passages. One more pass with the mill will get the deck true.

16 Mill as Needed

16–To get the deck really true, Grubbs goes one more pass with the milling machine.

17 Countersink Bores

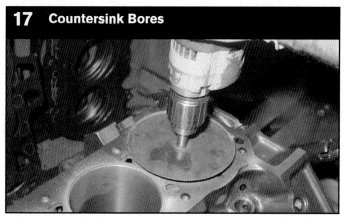

17–Each of the cylinder bores is countersunk for ease of piston installation when the time comes. This takes away sharp edges that can also cause detonation.

18 Chase Bolt Holes

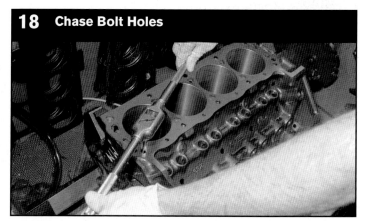

18–Grubbs believes in chasing and cleaning all bolt holes in the block to ensure smooth assembly. Jim uses WD-40 or cutting oil as a lubricant.

MASTER MECHANIC TIP

19 Hone Lifter Bores

19–Here is something not many of us think about when we're building an engine. Honing the lifter bores improves oil control and ensures smooth lifter movement. Take a look at this smooth crosshatch pattern.

20 Install the Block Dowels

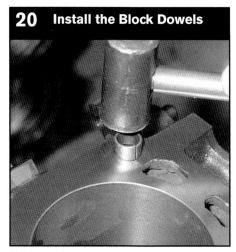

21 Get Ready to Hone

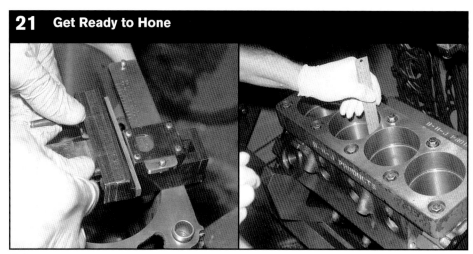

20–Install the block dowels and leave them in the block. You'll have to tap them into place.

21–We're going to hone the cylinder bores now. We hone the cylinders to give the walls a super-fine finish in the wake of boring. Grubbs sets up the hone for proper sizing. He also determines how much of the bore needs to be honed.

22 Time to Hone

22–Grubbs works the hone up and down, checking bore dimensions every so many passes. The objective is a 4.030-inch bore based on piston dimensions for each bore.

23 Inspect the Oil Galley Ports

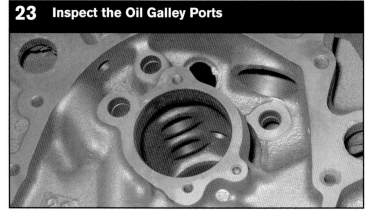

24 Tap Oil Galley Passages

23–Here's a close look at the front oil galley ports. Grubbs is going to tap these galleys and install screw-in plugs for security. Bolt holes need to be chased and lubricated during the machining process.

24–Front oil galley passages, which have a press-fit plug from the factory, get tapped for screw-in plugs. This is a wise move for any build-up.

25 Test Fit Plugs

25–*Oil galley plugs are screwed in as a test fit, then removed. We still have to wash the block, which means all freeze and galley plugs must be removed.*

26 Ready for Cleaning

26–*Our machined block is ready for a thorough cleaning. Grubbs has it up on the workbench for inspection and any repairs that need to be done.*

27 Clean the Block

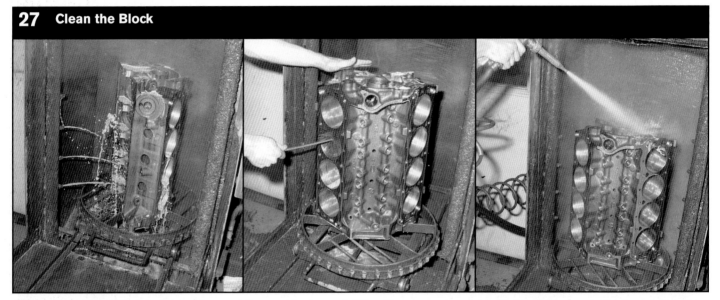

27–*The block is placed in the washer and thoroughly cleaned. Oil galley passages and cylinder walls are washed using brushes. This gets all of the grit and other debris out from the machining process.*

28 Dry the Block

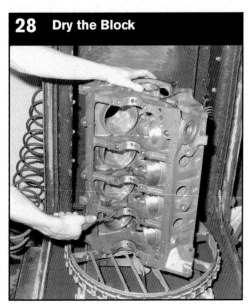

28–*Once out of the washer, the block is dried with compressed air. This removes moisture, which can cause rust. It also clears any debris from cooling system and oil passages.*

29 Coat the Cylinder Walls

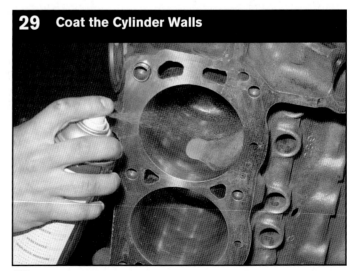

29–*WD-40 is sprayed on the cylinder walls and decks to prevent rust formation.*

30 Prepare the Cam Bearings

30–*Before you install the cam bearings, all five are inspected and dressed as shown. Sharp edges are removed as shown. This prevents scoring the cam journals.*

31 Install the Cam Bearings

31–*Cam bearing installation must be approached carefully – gently manipulate them into place without causing bearing damage. Oil holes must line up with the oil galley holes in the block.*

32 Line Up the Oil Holes

IMPORTANT STEP ❗

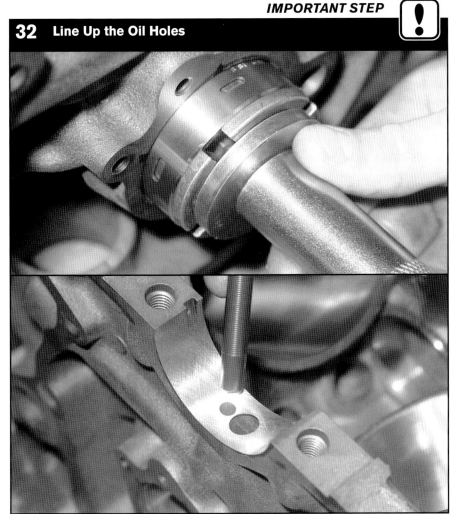

❗ *32*–*The number-1 cam bearing has two oil holes that must line up with the oil galleys in the block. If you forget this important fact, you will not have oil pressure to any part of the engine beyond the oil filter. You will have oil pressure at the sending unit, which will make it look like you have oil pressure. As the engine runs, void of oil pressure beyond the filter, moving parts are eating each other alive.*

33 Paint the Block

33–*The block is painted and readied for assembly. It will be mounted on an engine stand and wrapped in plastic to protect it from dust and debris.*

ROTATING ASSEMBLY

The bottom end – the crankshaft, connecting rods, and pistons – are what turn thermal energy into rotary motion – and power. These components are what make it happen when you turn the key. It's important that these components get close attention during the machining process.

With small-block Fords, you're going to be dealing with one of a handful of crankshaft types – the 1M (221/260/289), 2M (302 and 5.0L), or the 3M (351W). If your engine project happens to be a 351C, the 4M cast-iron crankshaft is what you can expect to find inside.

Crankshafts don't always have to be machined during a rebuild. Sometimes, you can get away with polishing the journals and installing standard main and rod bearings. This is determined by measuring each of the journals with a micrometer. In fact, our 289 short-block from Mustangs Etc., with 1960s vintage forged pistons, has a flawless 1M crankshaft that only needs polishing and standard bearings. Good for us. Bad for the crankshaft grinder.

When journals are scored or worn, the crankshaft will need to be machined at least .010-inch undersize at the journals involved. If the scoring is any deeper than .020-inch, we suggest replacement of the crankshaft. You can get away with a .030-inch undergrind on a mild-mannered street engine. But remember, for every .010-inch you grind off the journals, the weaker the crankshaft becomes. Going .010 and .020 inch undersize is normal. Going beyond .020 inch undersize is challenging fate. For all of the concern over going beyond .020 inch undersize, having to grind a crankshaft beyond that dimen-

Machining the Rotating Assembly

1   Examine the Crank

1–Crankshafts don't always need to be ground to the next undersize. Determine rod and main journal sizes, and then decide where you're going next. Scored crankshaft journals must be machined to the next undersize. Undamaged journals can often be polished, with the same size bearing. This saves money.

2   Remove the Pistons

2–Old pistons are pressed off the connecting rods. These were TRW period forged aluminum pistons from the 1960s.

IMPORTANT STEP ❗

3   Examine the Rods

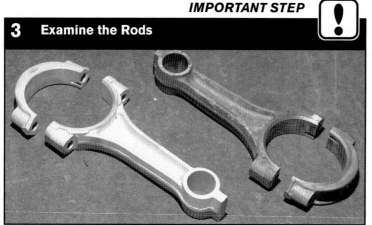

❗ *3–We are running C3AE connecting rod forgings in our 289. Here are two types of rod forgings side by side. On the left is a C3AE forging. On the right is the more common C8OE forging for the 302. It's hard to tell these forgings apart, but they're different. The C8OE forging is shorter and is intended for the 2M crankshaft with a 3.00-inch stroke. The C3AE forging is longer and intended for the 2.87-inch stroke.*

4   Deburr the Rods

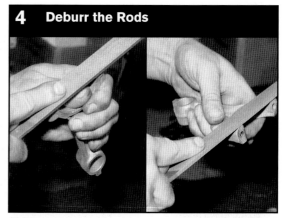

4–Connecting-rod reconditioning begins with a personal massage with a file. This process deburrs the rod, minimizing any chance of stress cracking or failure. It also ensures a better fit between the cap and rod.

sion is rare. Most crankshafts need to be turned .010 inch undersize.

While you're focused on the crankshaft, the oil holes need to be chamfered (beveled) to allow an improved oil flow to the bearings and journals. When we chamfer the oil holes, we open up the oil passage, increasing the volume. Any reputable machinist and engine builder understands how to do this. It is an affordable, important step in an engine build.

Another clause in your engine life insurance policy is to radius the connecting rod journals, which reduces stress and gives the bearing more surface area to lean on. This is common with aftermarket stroker kits. When we radius the journals, we are giving the bearing and the crankshaft a smoother marriage with big shoulders. Ask your machine shop about this step.

Unless you are going racing, shot-peening and nitriding (also known as tufftriding) are unnecessary for the crankshaft. If you expect to hammer your crankshaft hard, opt for an aftermarket bottom end starting with a nodular-iron or steel crankshaft. Nodular-iron cranks are excellent for weekend racers. If you expect to go road racing, use nitrous or supercharging, go with a steel crankshaft. Fast bolt-on horsepower doesn't come cheap. When you get 150 horsepower with the touch of a button, it has to come from somewhere. Nitrous oxide will hammer your crankshaft hard. So will a lot of supercharger boost. This is when a steel crankshaft is a must. The naturally aspirated weekend drag racer can get away with a nodular-iron crankshaft.

Small-block Fords have been blessed with good connecting rods dating back to those 221- and 260-ci small-blocks of 1962 to '64. All these dependable C3AE rods have done through the years is get better. In the old days, racers like Carroll Shelby, and Holman & Moody, didn't have aftermarket connecting rods at their disposal; they had to work with what the factory offered. So, they shot-

5 Mill the Big End

5–The large end of the rod is carefully milled for a perfect union with the cap. This gets the large end of the rod square.

6 Mill the Rod Cap

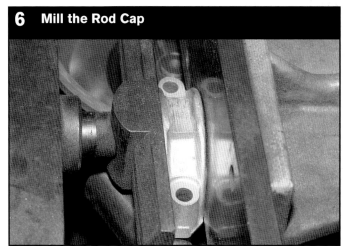

6–We do the same thing with the rod cap. It gets milled as shown for a perfect union with the rod.

7 Countersink Rod Bolt Holes

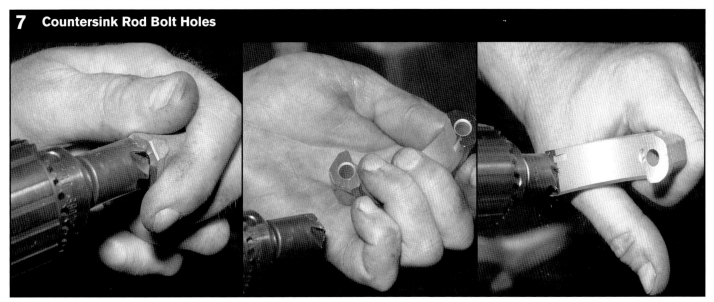

7–The connecting-rod bolt holes are countersunk for ease of bolt installation and to reduce stress issues.

8 Install the Rod Bolts

8–New 5/16-inch ARP rod bolts with the Wave-Loc design are installed. A press is used to press the bolts into the rod.

9 Lubricate the Threads

9–ARP assembly lube is used on the rod bolt threads for good, uniform torque readings.

TORQUING FASTENERS

10 Install the Nuts

10–The rod nuts are torqued to 19 to 25 ft-lbs.

11 Smooth the Rods

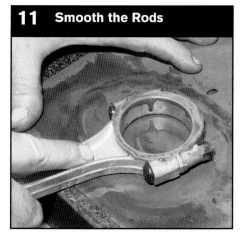

11–Each connecting rod is wet-worked over a 240-grit sheet of sandpaper. This dresses the sides of the rod journal for a smoother marriage with the crankshaft.

peened these connecting rods, fit them with 3/8-inch bolts, and spun those 289s to 8,000 rpm. Veteran engine builder John Da Luz of JMC Motorsports in San Diego, California, has built powerful small-block Fords using stock C3AE 289 and 302 rod forgings fitted with 3/8-inch bolts. We've watched these engines spin to 8,200 rpm with factory rods, so you can sleep comfortably with these connecting rods in your streetable small-block Ford.

Jim Grubbs Motorsports has taken our 289 rod forgings, cleaned them up, and reconditioned them. The rods are thoroughly inspected. Anything not quite up to snuff is tossed into the recycle barrel. Jim recommends matched connecting rods in a quality rebuild. This means we want connecting rod forgings that are of the same vintage and close to the same weight. That way we can grind them to the same exact weight during dynamic balancing. Rods that have already been ground down are of no value unless eight of them can be made to weigh the same.

You want to examine both ends of the rod to ascertain integrity. Look for evidence of damage from a spun bearing, for example. Any bluing from an overheated bearing is cause to throw one out. If you are having a tough time finding connecting rods for a 289, you may want to opt for aftermarket Crower Sportsman rods or change the entire bottom end out of a 302 with the 2M crank and rods, which are more common. Once it is all screwed together, no one will know it's a 302 but you.

When we recondition connecting rods, we do the same thing we did with the main bearing saddles in the block – resize the large end of the connecting rod. First, we disassemble the connecting rods, keeping each cap with each rod forging. We resize connecting rods because the large end of the rod becomes egg-shaped over time from rapid reciprocating motion. The harder we work an engine, the more pronounced this distortion becomes.

12 Rods are Assembled

12–*Eight C3AE rod forgings are ready for reconditioning.*

Resizing, or reconditioning, the connecting rod involves milling the cap and the rod, and then resizing the journal. When we get the journal back to its original size, we also create a crosshatch pattern, which helps keep the bearing secure. Reconditioning the rod also involves installing new bolts. You can stick with the 5/16-inch size Ford used to begin with, or you can go with a 3/8-inch bolt like Ford did with the Boss 302. If you intend to run the engine hard, we suggest shotpeening the rod and installing 3/8-inch ARP bolts. Take extra care to inspect the rod bolt holes once they are machined for the larger bolts. Make sure the forging isn't thin around the bolt holes.

The small end of the rod doesn't need much attention. Inspect it for bluing and other evidence of overheating. Toss the rod if any of this evidence exists. When you fit the pistons, make sure the pin fit is snug and solid.

PRECISION MEASUREMENT

13 Measure the Journals

13–*Before reconditioning, the rod journals are measured as shown. This determines how much machining will have to be done on the large end's inside diameter.*

14 Resize the Journals

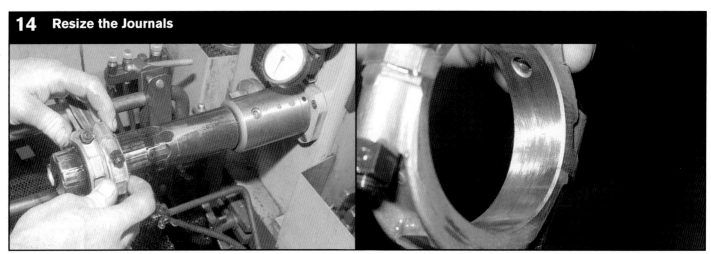

14–*Two rods, which share the same crankshaft journal, are machined as shown. Our goal here is to size the rods to factory specifications. This is the connecting rod bearing bore inside diameter – 2.2390 to 2.2398 inches. Reconditioned connecting rod journals should look like this – sized properly, with a nice crosshatch pattern for bearing security.*

MASTER MECHANIC TIP **PRO TIP**

15 Dynamic Balancing

PRO TIP **15**–*Dynamic balancing is the last phase of bottom-end machine work. It is here we determine how smoothly our engine will run. The pistons, rings, connecting rods, and even oil have to weigh the same as the crankshaft counterweights. We hang bobweights on the crankshaft rod journals to simulate piston, ring, and connecting-rod weight. Because the small-block Ford is externally balanced, we need the flywheel and harmonic balancer. Once we have established crankshaft weighting, we weigh each connecting rod and each piston/ring combination. We weigh every connecting rod to the lightest rod by removing material. With rods, we grind off iron at the small end and large end. Pistons are drilled beneath their crowns to get the weight down to the lightest slug.*

OIL SYSTEM

The small-block Ford has an adequate oiling system from the factory. Earlier, we mentioned chamfering crankshaft journal oil holes. We also mentioned chasing all of the oil galley passages. Most of us are guilty of taking a new oil pump out of the box and installing it in our engines without inspection. But, that's blind faith – and foolish. All oil pumps, unless purchased as "blueprinted" units, must be inspected before installation.

When you disassemble the pump, it's important to inspect rotor side clearances. Too much clearance means less pressure. Too little clearance can mean seizure. The pressure relief valve needs to be checked for freedom of movement against the spring. Wash the pump and its parts thoroughly. Then, reassemble and fill the cavity with 30-weight engine oil. One other suggestion is the use of a heavy-duty oil pump shaft for added security.

CYLINDER HEADS

The small-block Ford has never been blessed with particularly good cylinder heads in its half-century service life. Even the Boss 302 and 5.0L GT-40 were never impressive in the cylinder-head department. The Boss 302 was an excellent racing engine, but it was a real dog on the street because its huge ports didn't deliver good low-end torque. The 289 High Performance V-8 was a screamer, but never had enough cylinder head to pour on the torque at high RPM. The same can be said for the 5.0L Cobra GT-40 engine – not enough cylinder head to deliver the twist.

So, what to do about "Lo-Po" cylinder heads in the machine shop? John Da Luz of JMC Motorsports suggests good port and bowl work for improved torque. John has small-block Ford heads down to a science. He knows how to get these heads to flow impressive numbers with some hard and fast grinder work in his Southern California shop. John begins at the exhaust ports, which have a lot of room for improvement. Small-block Ford heads

Piston Forensics

When we got our 289 short-block from Mustangs Etc. in Van Nuys, California, we didn't know it had been rebuilt early in its service life. Inside were standard TRW forged pistons from the 1960s. Some of you may remember 1969 to '70 Boss 302 engines had issues with cracked piston skirts. This problem wasn't isolated to the Boss 302 engine alone. These pistons were purchased from the automotive aftermarket years before the Boss 302 engine was conceived. Check out the skirt cracking here.

suffer from serious exhaust port restriction issues. John begins by eliminating the thermactor "hump" in the roof of the port. Then he works the rest of the port. The size difference in the port is incredible. Before John begins his port work, the exhaust port has sharp angles that restrict flow. When John is finished, it becomes a straight, unrestricted shot from valve seat to header flange. If you are stepping up to 351W heads, a JMC port and bowl job will wake your heads up.

And one other thing: port and bowl work isn't suggested for the novice. Good head porting technique – understanding what it takes to achieve good port flow without getting into the water jackets – takes years of experience.

Our stock 289-ci small-block won't be getting port work. However, it will be getting substantial head work in order to improve reliability and function. Because the original core had been through a rather unconventional rebuild, the cylinder heads suffered damage as a result. This was the first time we had ever witnessed a set of intake valve seats that needed to be replaced because of excessive wear. During a previous rebuild, the valves were reground at such an angle that they wore into the iron valve seats. One of the guys at Grubbs commented that you could shave with these valves because they were so badly worn.

Jim Grubbs Motorsports proved to us that no cylinder head is beyond repair if you know what you're doing. All exhaust valve seats were replaced with hardened steel seats for reliable use with unleaded fuels. This is suggested anytime you are going to be driving a vehicle daily or expect hard use. Show cars and occasional weekend drivers do not need hardened exhaust valve seats, so you might be able to save some money there.

We're going to remove the pressed-in rocker-arm studs and install screw-in studs. Here are the four basic types of rocker-arm studs available for small-block Fords prior to 1978. From left to right are conventional hex-shoulder screw-in stud, shoulderless screw-in adjustable stud, shoulderless positive-stop stud, and the adjustable press-in stud.

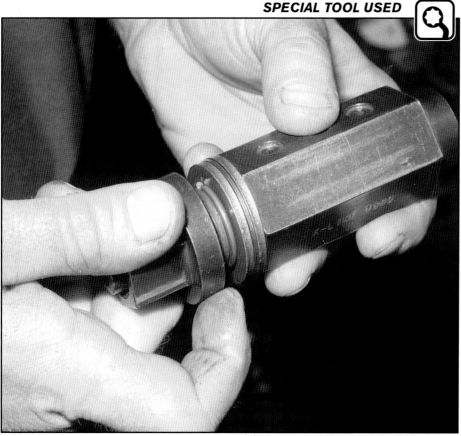

We're going to use this rocker-arm stud puller to remove the 16 pressed-in studs common with 1962 to '77 small-block Fords.

Our 289 heads also needed new valveguides. Because our heads suffered at the hands of a previous engine builder, some of the guides had to be completely replaced. Others needed only bronze inserts, which saved us money. Most rebuilds need only bronze valveguide inserts for solid reliability. If you want to begin factory fresh, you replace all 16 valveguides completely with oil-impregnated and knurled guides. Expect to spend a lot of money when you do, because valveguide replacement is time consuming.

A valve job should always include new valves. Old valves can be refaced to like-new condition and live 100,000 miles. However, valvestems cannot be reconditioned. New guides tend to take up the slack of worn valvestems. But, you tend to lose something along the way. New valves are cheap. They don't cost much more than about $10 each from Federal-Mogul's Speed Pro division. And, you can expect reliability

and peace of mind with 16 factory-fresh stopcocks. Spend the money – it's worth it.

Cylinder head refacing (milling) should be performed only if it is absolutely necessary. Each time we mill a cylinder head deck surface, we change a couple of things that are very important. We make the deck thinner, which adversely affects integrity. We also change the angle of the relationship between the heads and intake manifold, which can sometimes cause vacuum and coolant leak issues. As with the block, shave only the necessary amount off the head decks.

Another issue we were concerned with was rocker-arm studs. Our 289 had the original press-in studs. For stock engines with mild cam grinds, press-in studs work fine. If you are concerned about rocker-arm stud integrity, there are several solutions. One old hot-rodding trick is to "pin" the studs. Pinning the studs involves drilling a hole through the stud pedestal and inserting

a tension pin through the pedestal and stud. This keeps the stud "pinned" in the head.

An easier trick is to install screw-in rocker-arm studs. This may be performed several different ways. Jim Grubbs removed our press-in studs and installed screw-in studs. One downside to this idea is one problem we encountered where the studs back out of the head during valve lash adjustment. This mandated the use of poly-lock rocker-arm adjustment nuts, which is an unnecessary expense in our opinion on a stock engine. This is why we prefer the hex-shoulder, screw-in rocker-arm studs like we find with the 289 High Performance and Boss 302 engines.

There are three types of screw-in studs: adjustable, with a hex shoulder; adjustable, without a hex shoulder; and positive-stop, without the hex shoulder. The positive-stop, no adjust rocker-arm stud saw factory use from 1968 to '77. We suggest using adjustable, hex-shoulder, screw-in rocker-arm studs for best results. Always use Teflon sealer on the threads before screwing them into the cylinder head. This will keep coolant out of your oil.

If you're working with late-1966 through 1977 cylinder heads with rail-style rocker arms, it's best you have screw-in rocker-arm studs with pushrod guide plates installed. This is a great upgrade for high-performance applications. However, it's an important revision for just about any small-block Ford you happen to be building because it eliminates the troublesome rail-style rocker arm.

Another important upgrade is using improved valve seals instead of those umbrella seals we've been using since the beginning of time. Umbrella seals aren't happy with engine heat and oil. They become brittle, decay, and crumble, winding up in the oil pan pick-up. To install the improved valve seals, the cylinder head must be machined to fit the seal. This adds to the cost, but it improves longevity.

When it is time to install freeze plugs in the heads and block, always use brass – never steel. Steel freeze plugs corrode with time and use. Brass freeze plugs do not.

Machining the Heads

1   Remove Rocker-Arm Studs

1–The stud removal tool and an air impact wrench are used to extract each of the studs.

2   Measure the Stud Hole

2–The rocker-arm stud hole, which opens right into the water jacket, is measured to determine what sized tap we're going to need.

3   Tap the Hole

3–A tap is gently run into the hole to cut threads for the screw-in stud. In view of some of the problems we had with studs working loose, we suggest the hex-shoulder, adjustable rocker-arm studs like we find with the 289 High Performance V-8.

4   Check the Fit

4–Our rocker-arm stud holes are tapped and ready for a fit check. It screws in nice and smoothly. The stud will have to have Teflon sealer around the threads to keep coolant inside, but that will come later when the studs are permanently installed after the cylinder heads are cleaned.

5 Remove the Valveguides

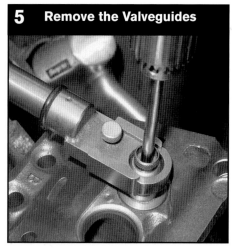

5–*Our 1965 289 cylinder head castings need a lot of attention due to inadequate engine building procedures in the past. First, we're going to ream out the bronze valveguides as shown.*

6 Install the Valveguides

6–*We're installing new Hastings bronze valveguide liners in these heads. The valvestem rides on this guide, which transfers heat and carries oil down the stem more effectively. Each of the bronze guides is driven into the valveguide as shown.*

7 Trim the Excess

7–*Once the guide is driven into place, the excess is trimmed off as shown.*

SPECIAL TOOL USED

8 Measure the Valvestem

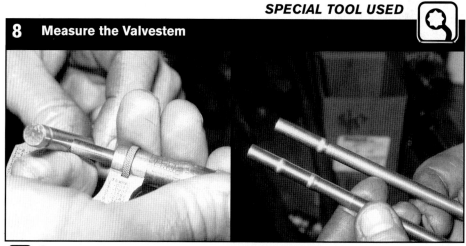

8–*Now, we have to measure the valvestem and machine the guides to fit. The tool we use to machine the guides is called a spiraling arbor.*

9 Resize the Guide

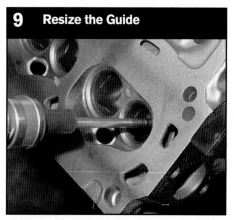

9–*The spiraling arbor is driven through the bronze liner, sizing the guide to the size of the valvestem and securing the liner into the guide.*

10 Trim the Guide

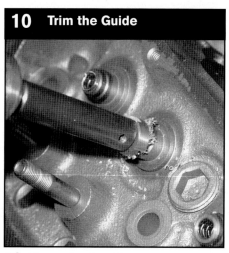

10–*The resized guide gets a trim job, machined flush as shown.*

11 Countersink the Guide

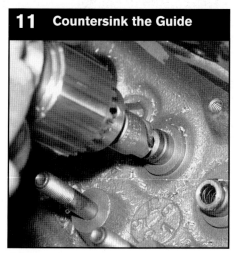

11–*The end of the guide is countersunk for a smooth valvestem transition.*

12 Test-Fit the Valves

12–Here, Grubbs sets up the dial-bore gauge for proper valvestem and guide sizing. The valvestem must slide smoothly, with a nice glide back and forth, without binding.

13 Hone the Valveguides

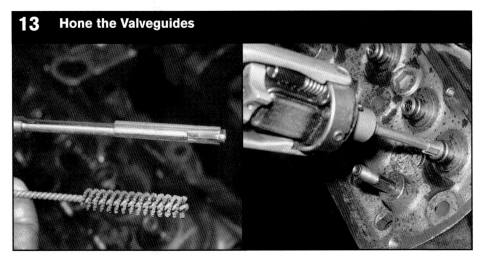

13–Here are two kinds of valveguide hones. On top, a conventional hone. On the bottom, a ball hone. Which one your machine shop uses is a matter of personal preference. The conventional hone is more expensive, but it does a better job. We're going to use a valveguide hone to put a nice finish on the bronze inserts for good oil control and proper sizing.

14 Observe the Results

14–Observe these two valveguides. The guide on the right has been honed while the guide on the left hasn't been touched yet. The crosshatch pattern on the right makes the bronze guide dull, which will help oil control.

15 Prepare for the Valve Seal

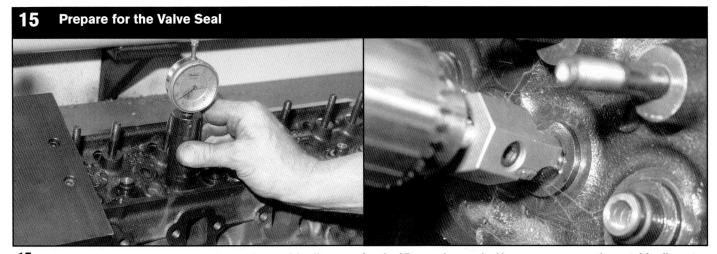

15–We're getting ready to cut the valveguide outside diameter for the Viton valve seals. Here, we measure the outside diameter to determine what sized cutter we're going to use. Then the outside diameter of the valveguide is cut to fit the Viton valve seal. The Viton seal is better than the Teflon seal, and remarkably better than the umbrella seals we find inside a lot of these engines.

16 Install the Valve Seal

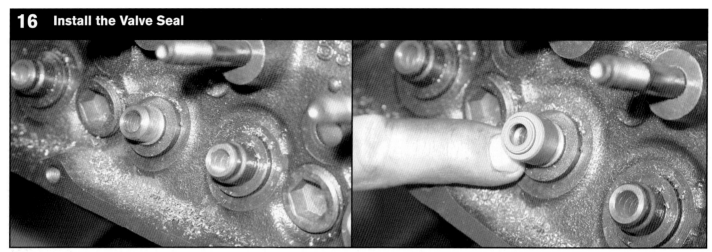

16–*The machined valveguide on the left is ready for its Viton seal. Note the difference from the unmachined guide on the right. In the second photo, the valve seal has been installed (finger). This is a nice seal because it outlasts virtually everything in the marketplace. It maintains a snug fit around the valvestem, which means good oil control for your new engine.*

MASTER MECHANIC TIP *PRO TIP*

17 Exhaust Valve Seats

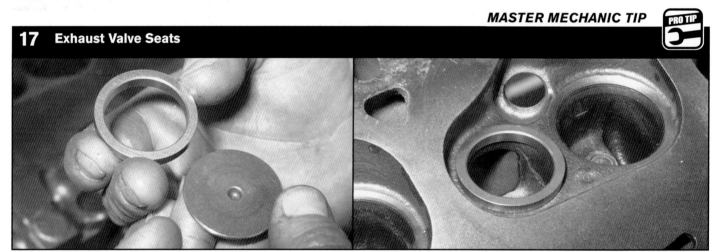

17–*Hardened valve seats should be your next consideration after valveguide replacement. Hardened valve seats became important when tetraethyl lead was removed from automotive fuels in the 1980s. Weekend cruisers and tailored show cars do not need hardened exhaust valve seats; daily drivers and weekend racers do. We're going to cut out the iron exhaust valve seat and install this hardened seat.*

18 Prepare the Valve Seats

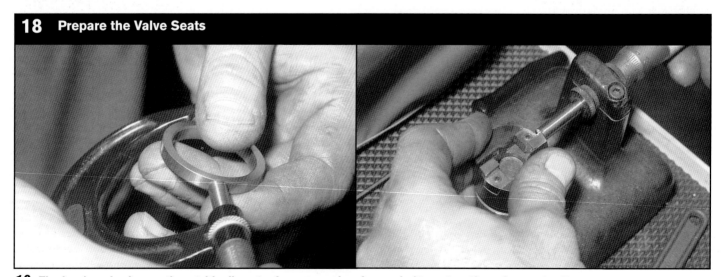

18–*The hardened valve seat's outside diameter is measured and recorded to set up the valve-seat cutter.*

19 Prepare the Head

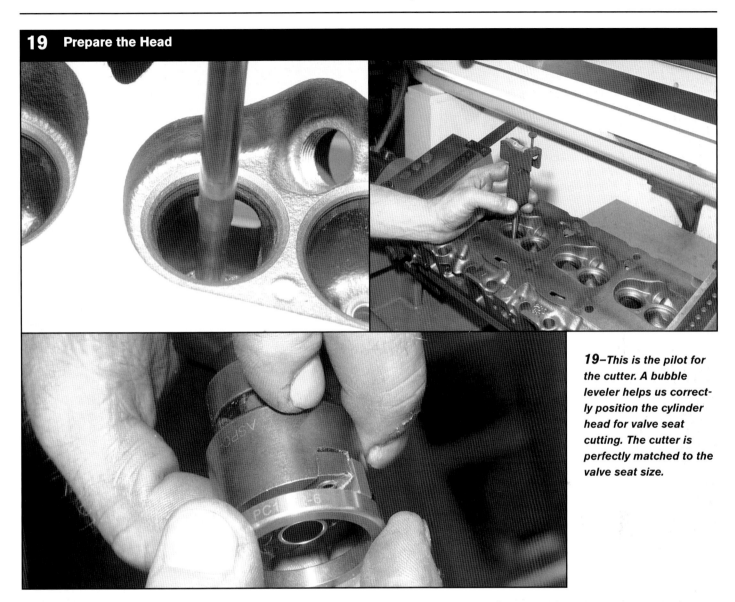

19–This is the pilot for the cutter. A bubble leveler helps us correctly position the cylinder head for valve seat cutting. The cutter is perfectly matched to the valve seat size.

20 Measure the Valve Seat

20–Here, we measure the thickness of the valve seat, which helps determine how deep we're going to cut the cylinder head for valve-seat placement. The old iron valve seat has been cut out, making way for the steel valve-seat insert. The old iron seat was actually part of the iron casting. Iron doesn't wear as well as hardened steel. Steel valve seats are installed in cast-aluminum heads as well.

21 Install the Valve Seat

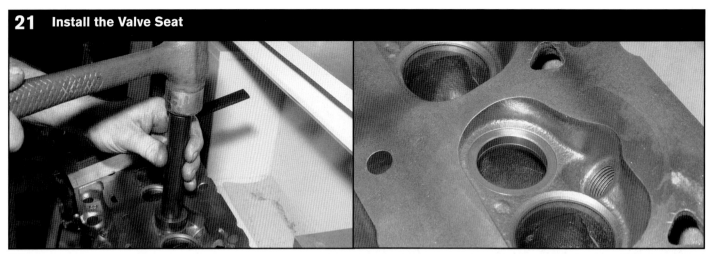

21–*The hardened exhaust valve seat is driven into place. Once installed, the exhaust valve seat looks like this. It still has to be ground to mate properly with the valve head.*

22–*Close inspection of the intake-valve iron seat shows the result of a poor valve job. The intake valve wore its way deep into the iron seat. When valve seating becomes a problem, we have to install hardened intake valve seats.*

22 Intake Valve Seats

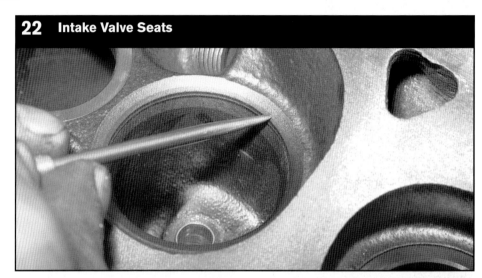

Crack Checking

WORKBENCH TIP

Before you commit any time and money to a casting, have your machine shop do a magnetic particle inspection. A bright yellow medium, which just happens to be magnetic, is sprinkled on the iron casting as shown. When we apply a magnetic field, this draws the yellow particles to any cracks in the iron, which become immediately apparent if there's a crack.

23 Look at the Valve

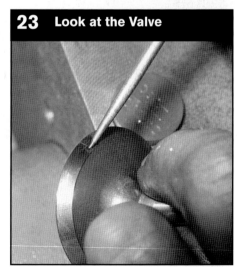

23–*A "valve job" involves shaping the valves and seat so they fit together and seal perfectly. The valve should seat smack in the middle of the machined face as shown.*

24 Grinding the Intake Seat

24–*Bench racers like to brag about three-angle valve jobs. But, a three-angle valve job is just common sense. A three-angle cut distributes the load more evenly across the valve face and seat. It also offers improved airflow through the port and across the valve seat. Some machine shops make three separate cuts to achieve three angles. Jim Grubbs Motorsports has a cutter that does all three angles at the same time.*

25 Grind the Exhaust Seat

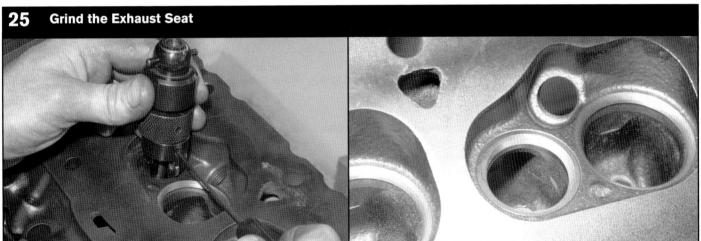

25–*Once the guide is driven into place, the excess is trimmed off as shown.*

26 Test Fit the Valves

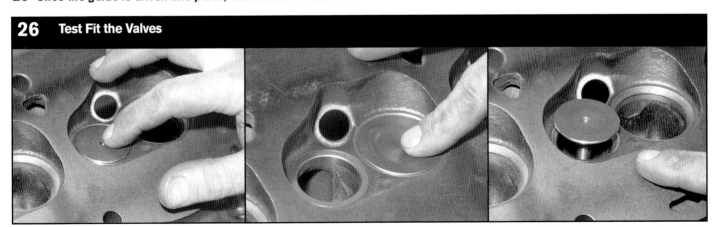

26–*The intake and exhaust valves are checked for proper seating. We'll get more into proper valve seating in the text ahead. As you can see, the three-angle valve job allows air to flow smoothly across the seat and valve face.*

27 Examine the Angles

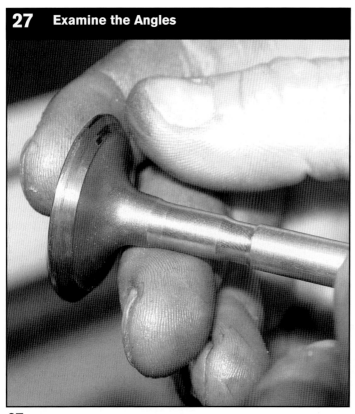

27–When we rub the valve face into the freshly ground seat, it scribes a line in the valve face. This shows us where the valve contacts the seat. Later, we'll grind the valves to match the new seats.

29 Wash the Heads

28 Mill the Heads

28–With valve and seat work finally out of the way, we are ready to mill the head deck surfaces. The head is set up on the mill. Our approach here needs to be the same as it was with the block deck. Each head is milled a few thousandths at a time, checking to see where the irregularities are. We shave just enough to get the deck level – and no more.

29–With all machining work completed, the cylinder heads are washed with the same diligence as the block.

30 Mark the Valves

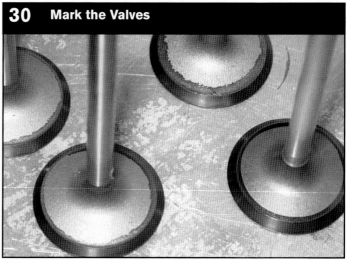

30–A red dye is painted on the valve faces. This dye is there to show us where we have ground the valve faces.

31 Grind the Valves

31–Valve grinding is the same as it has always been. We grind the face at a specific angle designed to fit the three-angle seat.

32 Lubricate the Valvestems

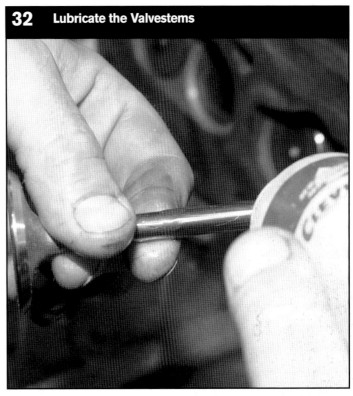

32–Valvestems are lubricated with engine assembly lube prior to installation.

33 Find Valvespring Height

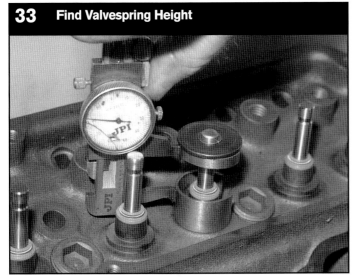

33–The valvespring installed height is determined next.

34 Determine Spring Pressure

34–Spring pressure is determined next. Then, we dial in the spring pressure at the valve using shims.

35   Install Springs, Retainers, and Keepers

36   Check Valve Seating

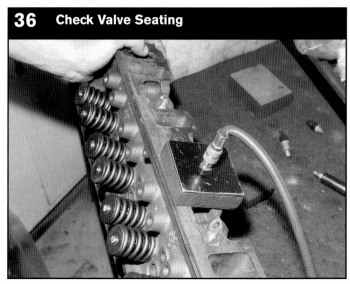

35–The valvesprings, retainers, and keepers are installed next. Proper seating of the keepers and retainers is ascertained by tapping the keeper with a hammer.

36–We check proper valve seating by applying vacuum at each of the ports. If the vacuum holds, we have excellent valve seating.

37   Install Rocker-Arm Studs

37–Screw-in, adjustable-rocker-arm studs are installed next. Teflon sealer is used on these studs. Torque these studs to 35 ft-lbs. Use Poly-Loc adjustment nuts.

When Valveguides are Beyond Repair

WORKBENCH TIP

What to do when the original iron valveguides are so far gone they cannot be repaired? Most of the time, we can install bronze liners to infuse new life into old, worn-out valveguides. This approach worked quite well for most of our cylinder head work. However, we had one guide that was damaged beyond repair. Here's what we did.

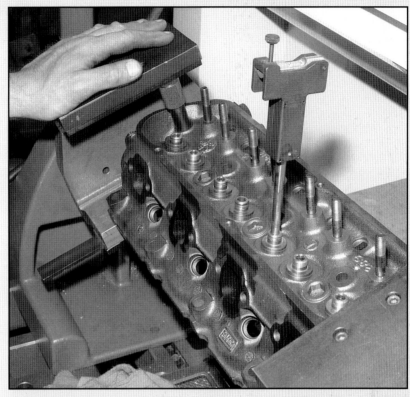

First, we set the cylinder head up on the bench for accurate machining. You wouldn't want a valveguide that was slightly out of plumb with the cylinder head. Don't laugh – it happens at better machine shops everywhere.

Did you know you can buy new steel valveguides for virtually any cylinder head in existence? All we have to do is bore out the old guide and drive in the new one.

The old valveguide is reamed out as shown, leaving a shell.

This ream does a finer cut, which will give the new valveguide something to hang onto.

When Valveguides are
Beyond Repair (continued)

This is what the machined valveguide bore looks like.

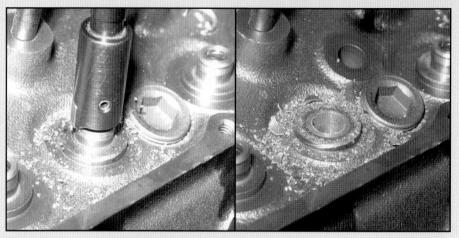

The shell is machined down to the surface of the head. This isn't a mandatory step, but it cleans the surface up nicely.

A close look at the port shows it is cracked around the guide bore. This can be welded up and machined smooth. This crack indicates intense heat in port area.

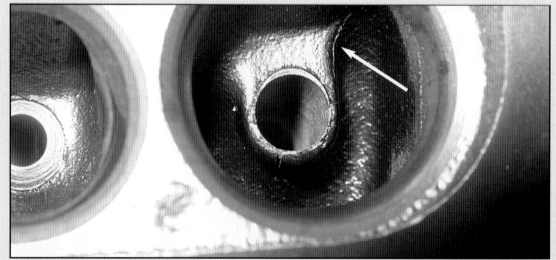

The valveguide bore gets a countersinking for easy installation of the new guide.

The new guide is driven into place with an impact gun.

When Valveguides are
Beyond Repair (continued)

Because replacement guides aren't always the same length as originals, we wind up with more guide than we need.

The new guide is machined down to the proper height.

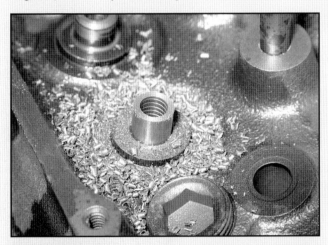

This is what the guide looks like once it is machined to the correct height. There's still more work to do here. This is a knurled guide. We can machine the inside of the guide for our valvestems. And, we can even install a bronze insert to get it identical to the 15 other guides with bronze inserts.

The top of the guide is machined to properly fit the Viton seal.

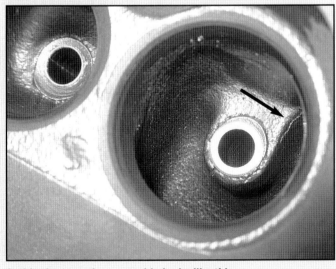

Inside the port, the new guide looks like this.

You may also purchase replacement valveguides that already have the bronze liner installed inside. This eliminates the bronze-liner installation process.

ENGINE ASSEMBLY

Assembling an engine is likely the most exciting segment of engine building. This is where we put our hands on all of an engine's components and set them into productive motion. But, to put them into a productive, power-making motion, we have to assemble them properly, and with painstaking detail.

Before assembly begins, we need to houseclean, with all components clean and laid out in proper assembly order. It's a good idea to wash down everything with a solvent to remove all dust and debris. Brake cleaner is a good cleaning solvent, as is the solvent we use in parts washers. If you're using a parts washer, you want fresh solvent; don't use dirty solvent.

It is very important to keep pistons and connecting rods in proper order to avoid mismatches. Since each piston has been sized to each bore, we don't want to make the mistake of installing pistons in the wrong bores. This is also important for the sake of dynamic balancing.

Engine parts, centered around the crankshaft, need to be set up on the work bench. Pistons and rods need to be laid out around their respective posi-

tions on the crank. The oil pump and driveshaft need to be parked off to the side. Main caps should be bolted to the block in their respective positions. At this point, our block and heads need to be ready for assembly. Heads, especially, should be completely assembled, ready to bolt on.

The block needs to be safely mounted on an engine stand that allows you to rotate it 360 degrees. This enables you to rotate the block as you install the crank and assemble the bottom end. We discourage building the engine on a workbench, which a good

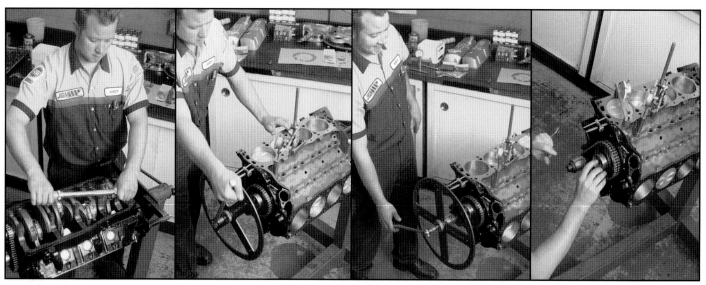

Now for the fun part – but don't get too excited and mess something up. Take your time and do it right the first time.

Building in Power

WORKBENCH TIP

When we're planning for power, we don't always stop to consider how power gets wasted in an engine's design and construction. Friction is the power pick-pocket hiding in all sorts of places inside our engines. Most friction occurs at the pistons and rings; some comes from bearings and journals; and even more is produced between the pistons and piston wrist pins, lifters and bores, cam lobes and lifters, and rocker-arm fulcrums and valvestems.

During the engine build, our goal needs to be compromise between having tolerances that are too loose and too tight. Piston-to-cylinder-wall clearances are critical in order to have good cylinder sealing, without too much friction and drag. The same is true for rod and main bearing clearances.

Another power-waste issue is engine breathing. You want an induction system that helps your engine breathe well at the RPM range it is designed and built for. This means the appropriate intake manifold and carburetor. Go too small on carburetor sizing

and you restrict breathing. If ports don't match in terms of size, you restrict breathing. Opt for cylinder heads where port sizing is too limited for your displacement and you restrict breathing. One example would be stock 289/302 heads on a 355-ci stroker. This brings compression to mind immediately. Run too much compression and you kill power (and the engine!) through detonation.

On the exhaust side, you want a scavenging system that makes sense. You don't have to have long-tube headers for great breathing. Shorty headers will do the job just as well, and without the shortcomings of long-tube headers. Go too large on header tube size and you hurt torque. Go too small and you hurt power on the high end. This is where your exhaust system has to work hand-in-hand with the heads, camshaft, and induction system. For more information on how to build performance in each of these areas, check out the other books in the CarTech® Books lineup.

---

many of us do when resources aren't available. Because engine stands are very inexpensive these days, it makes sense to buy one.

SHORT BLOCK

Short-block assembly should begin with the camshaft for ease of installation. Install the camshaft first because the crankshaft won't be in the way. We can guide the cam through its journals more easily when we can get our hands in there. It's so easy to nick the bearings and create new problems if we can't guide the camshaft. Cam journals get a dose of engine assembly lube. Flat-tappet cam lobes get molybdenum grease – a thick

moly-coat lubricant that aids camshaft break-in during that first firing. Do not use molybdenum on the cam journals.

Roller-tappet camshafts get engine assembly lube on both the journals and lobes during installation. The same is true for the roller tappets when they're installed. Use lots of engine assembly lube on the lifters and rollers for best results.

With freshly machined main saddles, the main bearings should fit comfortably and stay put. Some builders lubricate the main saddles prior to bearing installation, which is just wrong. Main and rod bearings need a firm grip at the saddles and journals. When they don't have a firm grip, they can wrap themselves around the main and rod

journals, causing extensive damage and engine failure.

There is more to installing main bearings than fitting bearing halves into the saddles. We have witnessed main and rod-bearing failure for reasons most of us never think about. For example, if a piece of dirt or grit gets in between the bearing and saddle, it distorts the shape of the bearing, even when this debris is very small. This distortion causes the bearing surface to rise up against the crankshaft journal, causing a pressure point and premature bearing and crank wear. The high spot, that pressure point on the back of the bearing, wears first, wearing down to the copper. Once wear finds its way into the copper, crankshaft journal wear accelerates. This is why bearings must fit perfectly in the saddles and rod journals.

Before you lay the crankshaft in place, it's a good idea to thoroughly wash the crank, including oil passages, using a rat-tail wire brush. If you've already done this – do it again. This dislodges any stray particles that may have been missed during initial clean up after machine work. Once clean up is accomplished, we suggest measuring the crank journals one more time to confirm proper bearing sizing before installation.

When it's time to lay the crank in place, use an abundance of engine assembly lube on the bearings. The reason for this is simple: With the best-laid plans, engines sometimes go for months and even years before they're installed in a vehicle. Bearings and journals need plenty of lubrication during "sit" time. And when it's time to fire the engine, oil system priming is suggested as a life insurance policy against friction during start-up. We'll get into that in Chapter 6.

Main cap installation is an area that really mandates your close attention. With the crank in place and main caps snugged (but not torqued), check crankshaft end-play and side clearances. Main bearing caps are numbered from the front of the block as #1 through #5. Torque the #3 cap first, then #2, then #3, then #1, then #5 for best results. Torque the main caps in third or half values. Don't torque the main caps all at once to the specified torque. Take it slowly and methodically. Then, check end-play and side clearances again.

With pistons pressed on the connecting rods, we're ready to install the rings. Pistons rings need to be installed with a lot of forethought. First, they need to be rolled onto the piston without scratching the aluminum. Ring end gaps should be positioned around the piston in quarters – 9, 12, 3, and 6 o'clock. Piston-ring compressors come in a variety of types. Adjustable, worm-gear piston ring compressors are the most common type, available at Harbor Freight or your nearest tool equipment store. You can buy a ring compressor, or you can rent one, depending on how often you intend to build engines. Billet, bore-size-specific ring compressors are the easiest type to use. However, they are the most expensive. Billet ring compressors are common in better machine shops everywhere because they are used so often.

Goin' Fishing

WORKBENCH TIP

John Da Luz of JMC Motorsports recommends a fish scale to determine how tight things are in the cylinder bore. Before you install pistons and rods, ring the pistons and insert each of them in the bore one at a time. Hook a fish scale around the wrist pin and pull on the piston. If it takes more than eight pounds to pull the piston up the bore, clearances are too tight.

Piston-to-cylinder-wall clearances get the final check with a fish scale. If it takes more than eight pounds to pull the piston out of the bore, clearances are too tight. This test is performed with the piston rings installed.

When Bearing Clearances Won't Jibe

WORKBENCH TIP

During an engine build we were undertaking for *How to Build Big-Inch Ford Small-Blocks*, also available from CarTech® books, we learned something valuable from John Da Luz of JMC Motorsports. John was building a 331-ci stroker for a customer, and crankshaft end-play came in tight. John could have taken the crankshaft to a machine shop and had the thrust journal machined. Instead, he chose to sand the thrust bearing as shown on a piece of plate glass. The plate glass offers a perfect surface to work the bearing's thrust surfaces. John was able to remove just enough aluminum from the bearing surfaces to get the clearances he was seeking.

MASTER MECHANIC TIP

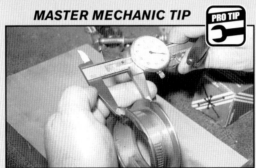

John Da Luz mikes the thrust bearing sides after checking crankshaft end-play. It looks like he needs to remove a little material.

John works the sides of the thrust bearing using a piece of 240-grit paper. He removes a little bit from each side.

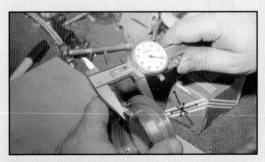

John rechecks the sides to see how much material he has removed.

John does the math and figures out how much he still needs to remove without harming the thrust bearing. When he's finished, he'll reinstall the crank and check end-play.

Cylinder walls need to be lubricated with engine assembly lube or 30-weight engine oil. Give the rings and piston skirts a dressing of assembly lube or engine oil as well. Both steps give pistons, rings, and cylinder walls lubrication for initial fire-up.

John Da Luz of JMC Motorsports suggests the fish-scale approach to checking piston-to-cylinder fit. If it takes more than eight pounds of force to pull the piston through the bore, your piston-to-cylinder-wall clearances are too tight. This can also mean ring end gap is too small. Don't chance it – go back and check these issues.

When you are installing pistons and rods, the rod bolts need to be covered with rod-bolt condoms, which prevent damage to rod journals and cylinder walls. Even with this protection in place, you need to carefully guide each piston and rod carefully into the bore. Take extra care to ensure the rod and bearing seat properly onto the rod journal. Make sure the bearing is installed properly on the rod, with the tang seated in the slot on the rod. You would be amazed how many of us get this backwards. It is costly when it happens.

Hand-tighten the rod bolts and check side clearances before torquing the rod bolts to specs. Each time you install a piston and rod, hand-crank the engine to check resistance. With all eight pistons installed, you should be able to turn the crankshaft using a 1/2-inch drive breaker bar and two fingers at the end of the breaker bar. Checking resistance each time you install a rod and piston enables you to know quickly where the problem is. Torque the rod bolts, then go back and check rod bolt torque again. Do this one rod journal, and two rods, at a time.

Timing set installation follows cam and crank installation, positioning the timing marks at 12 and 6 o'clock, respectively. We ran into a problem with our flat-tappet hydraulic camshaft from Federal-Mogul. The cam lobes were ever so slightly out of phase, which showed up when we were degreeing the cam. This meant our valve timing was a bit off and could adversely affect power.

Blueprinting an Oil Pump

WORKBENCH TIP

Thousands of engine builders install oil pumps every day right out of the box, and most of them enjoy success. But what if you received a defective oil pump and didn't know it until you fired the engine? Oil pumps should always be disassembled and checked thoroughly before being installed on your engine. Side clearances need to be checked, and the oil pressure relief valve needs to be checked for proper operation. Take these steps and sleep easier.

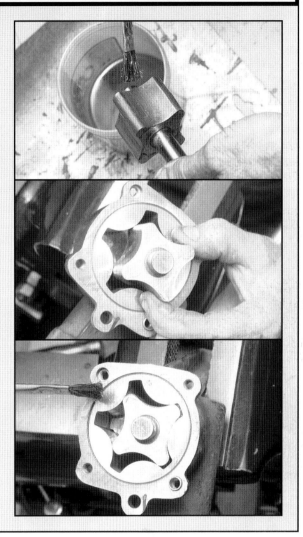

Basic Torque Specifications

Item	Torque Specifications
Main Bearing Caps	60-70 ft-lbs
Connecting Rods	40-45 ft-lbs
Cam Retainer Plate	6-9 ft-lbs
Cam Sprocket	40-45 ft-lbs
Harmonic Balancer	70-90 ft-lbs
Water Pump	12-15 ft-lbs
Cylinder Head Bolts	50, 60, and 65-72 ft-lbs
Intake Manifold	20-22 ft-lbs
Oil Pan	9-11 ft-lbs / 18 ft-lbs at timing cover and rear main
Flywheel	75-85 ft-lbs
Valve Covers	3-5 ft-lbs
Thermostat Housing	12-15 ft-lbs

This is when Jim Grubbs Motorsports decided to install a double-roller timing set where the valve timing could be corrected. This is why we show you a standard timing chain being installed, and a double-roller set later in this chapter.

WHY DEGREE A CAMSHAFT?

Making power isn't just about a longer stroke, large-port heads, big carburetor, and a lumpy camshaft; it's about the science of setting up your engine properly. Why do we degree camshafts after they're installed inside an engine? What does it accomplish?

Assemble the Short Block

1 **Inspect the Block**

1–Last-minute detailing is done on the block mating surfaces. A razor blade is used to debunk deck surfaces contaminated with paint and rust. Close inspection of the coolant and oil passages is good measure prior to assembly.

2 **It's Ready for Assembly**

2–The small-block Ford has five main bearings, with the thrust bearing at the number-3 journal. Small-block Chevrolets, by contrast, have the thrust bearing at the number-5 rear main bearing. Obviously, the main caps will have to be removed to install the crankshaft.

IMPORTANT STEP

3 **Install Oil Galley and Freeze Plugs**

3–Screw-in oil galley plugs are installed at this time prior to block assembly. We do these first to avoid any chance of forgetting. Teflon sealer or Permatex is used on these plugs to ensure a tight seal. There are three plugs at the front of the block behind the timing set. Freeze plugs also go in using silicone sealer around the perimeters. Don't forget the oil galley plug at the top of the block. There is no need for sealer here; just score the edges for security.

4 Wash the Cam

4–*The camshaft should be installed first because the crankshaft tends to get in the way of easy installation. Wash the cam thoroughly in solvent to remove all machining debris.*

Degreeing a camshaft is like a Columbo investigation. Call it, "just one more thing, Sir…" in your quest to learn the truth about power. The most basic reason for degreeing a camshaft is to determine that you have the correct grind for the job. Camshaft grinders today employ the most advanced technology available. As a result, few faulty camshafts ever make it to the consumer. However, camshafts do get mispackaged at times, which means you could receive a completely different grind than appears on the cam card and packaging. All the more reason to degree the cam going in.

We degree a camshaft by bolting a degree wheel to the crankshaft, cranking number-1 piston to top dead center (TDC), and installing a timing pointer. You can get a degree wheel from Comp Cams, Crane Cams, Performance Automotive Warehouse, and any number of other performance shops across the country. The bigger the wheel, the more accurate readings you'll get.

IMPORTANT STEP ❗

5 Lubricate the Cam Lobes

❗ **5**–*When you are installing a conventional flat-tappet camshaft, you need to use two different types of lubrication. The journals get engine assembly lube. The lobes get the molybdenum grease shown here. Do not get the molybdenum on the journals.*

6 Install the Cam

6–*The camshaft is carefully inserted into the cam alley, taking extra care to ensure that the journals are not nicked by the lobes.*

7 Install the Thrust Plate

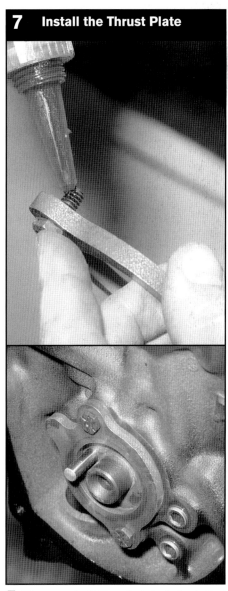

7–*The camshaft thrust plate is installed next using Loctite on the bolt threads for security. The oil passages on the thrust plate face the camshaft.*

8 Bearings into Caps

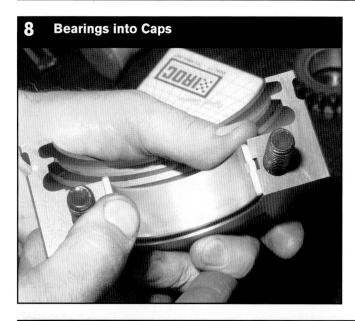

8–Main bearing halves are seated in the main caps. Bearings are installed in the caps dry, with no lubrication between the bearing and cap. Note proper positioning of the bearing tang or tab, which retains the bearing.

9 Remove Rope Seal Pin

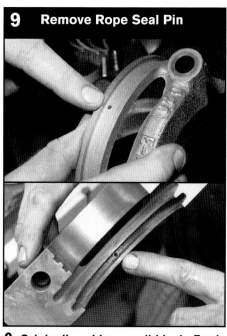

9–Originally, older small-block Fords had rope seals for rear main seals. Those old rope seals were retained with this pin. Replacement rubber seals don't need this pin. Unless you're using rope seals (which is not recommended), remove this pin. This pin will distort the rubber seal and cause an oil leak.

10 Thrust Bearing into Cap

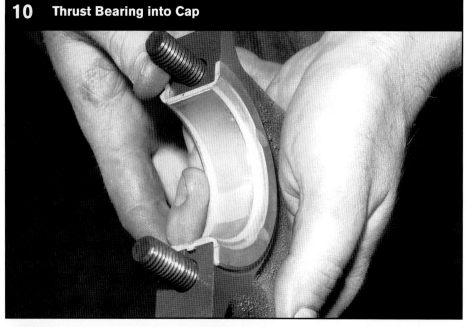

10–The main thrust bearing (number-3 saddle) is installed as shown in the main cap. This is called the thrust bearing because it keeps the crankshaft from "thrusting" fore or aft. It keeps the crankshaft centered in the block.

11 Bearings into Block

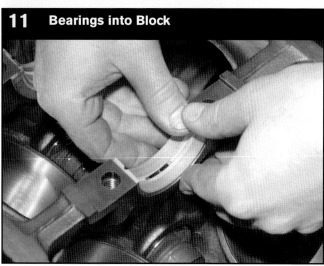

11–Main bearing halves are installed in the block next. As with the main caps, bearings go in dry for a firm grip.

12 Thrust Bearing into Block

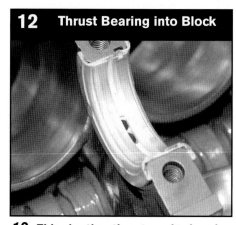

12–This is the thrust main bearing installed. Note the proper location of oil passages.

13 Install Rear Main Seal

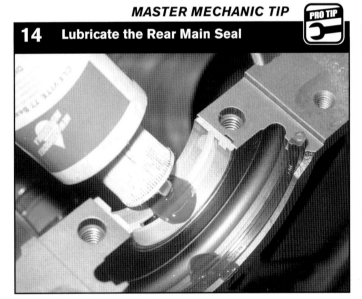

13—The rear main seal is next – installed as shown. Use a light film of silicone sealer between the seal and block. Don't use too much sealer – just a light touch. Note how the seal lip faces. It must be on the inside to ensure a positive seal. The seal tab should be outside. Jim Grubbs Motorsports positions the seal gaps away from the main cap gaps, which prevents leakage.

We find TDC with a bolt-on piston stop that screws into the spark plug hole or at the top of the block with the head removed. We suggest doing this with the cylinder head removed, which provides the greatest accuracy. Begin this process by turning the crankshaft clockwise until number-1 piston comes up to TDC. With the cylinder head installed, hold your thumb over the spark plug hole and listen to the air being forced out by the piston. The air will stop when you reach TDC.

At this point, both timing marks on the crank and camshaft sprockets should be in alignment at 12 and 6 o'clock. Install the degree wheel next and align the bolt-on timing pointer. With all of this accomplished, the number-1 piston should be at TDC, with the degree wheel and pointer at zero degrees. This becomes our base point of reference. Everything from here on out becomes BTDC (before top dead center) or ATDC (after top dead center). The intake valve will open at a given number of degrees ATDC and close at a given number of degrees BTDC. The exhaust valve will open at a given number of degrees BTDC and close at a given number of degrees ATDC. Much of this depends on valve overlap.

MASTER MECHANIC TIP

14 Lubricate the Rear Main Seal

14—The rear main seal gets liberal doses of engine oil or engine assembly lube. Put a dab of silicone sealer at the seal gaps before crank and bearing-cap installation. Don't forget to use plenty of engine assembly lube on all main bearing surfaces.

15 Set the Crank in Place

15—The 1M 2.87-inch stroke cast-iron crankshaft is lowered into place.

16 Prevent Leaks

16—Silicone sealer is used here at the rear main seal gaps to prevent leakage.

17 Lubricate the Main Threads

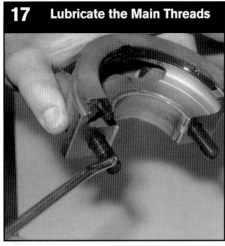

17–Main bolt threads should be lubricated with engine oil to ensure an accurate torque reading.

18 Install the Caps

18–Main bearings are lubricated with engine assembly lube and the caps installed as shown. Hand-tighten each cap, then snug with a socket wrench until the cap seats with the block.

19 Install the Rear Main

19–The rear main cap (number-5) is carefully seated in place. This one needs extra caution to ensure rear main seal security and smooth operation.

20 Torque the Main Caps

20–Main bearing cap bolts are torqued in third values – meaning they are torqued to one-third their full torque valve, then another third, then the full amount, which is 60 to 70 ft-lbs.

21 Check End-Play

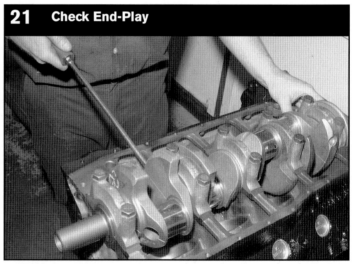

21–Crankshaft end-play should be .004 to .008 inch, checked with a dial-indicator (not shown here).

22 Install the Timing Set

22–The timing set is installed by sliding both sprockets and the chain on as a set. Timing marks in each of the sprockets are aligned at 12 and 6 o'clock to confirm proper valve timing.

23 Install the Pump Eccentric

23–For small-block Fords equipped with a mechanical fuel pump and carburetor, you'll have to install a fuel pump eccentric. Torque the bolt to 40 to 45 ft-lbs.

24 **Check Ring End Gaps**

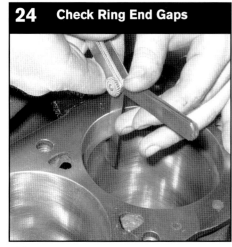

24–*Compression-ring end gaps should always be checked, even when you have pre-gapped piston rings. End gap should be .010 to .020 inch on both rings.*

25 **Second Ring**

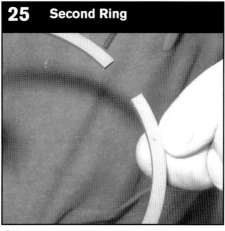

25–*Compression rings differ from each other based on the conditions they face. The top ring is exposed to more heat than the second ring. This is the second ring, identified with a dot.*

26 **Top Rings**

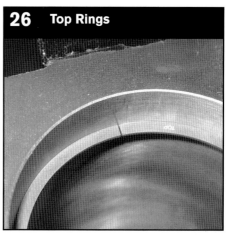

26–*The top compression ring is identified by the word "TOP" as shown. This varies from ring manufacturer to ring manufacturer. Check your instructions and the packaging for specifics.*

27 **Install the Expander**

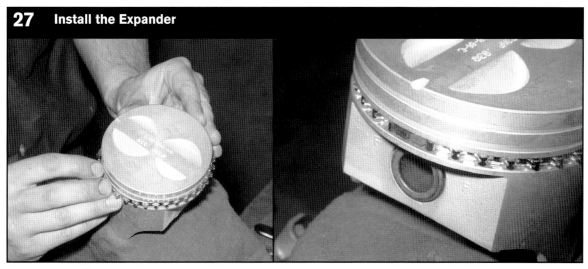

27–*Oil ring installation begins with the expander. Ends must meet as shown and not be overlapped.*

28 **Install the Oil Rings**

28–*Walk each of the oil rings onto the piston as shown. Position the end gaps 180 degrees opposite one another.*

29   Install the Compression Rings

29–The compression rings are installed next. Begin with the second ring, then the top ring. Make sure each ring is right-side up. You may roll the rings onto the piston by locking one end of the ring in the groove and walking the ring around into place. Take extra care not to scratch the ring lands. Here we're using a piston ring expander to install the ring.

30   Remove the Rod Nuts

30–All connecting-rod nuts are removed at this time. Do not remove the cap until it is time to install the piston and rod. This minimizes the risk of mixing up the rod caps, which are each matched to their rod.

31   Lubricate Bearings and Bolts

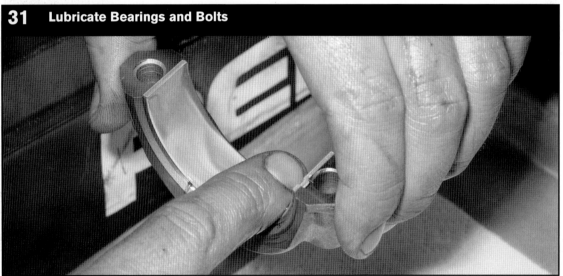

31–Lubricate the connecting rod bearing with assembly lube. Put a thin film of engine oil on the rod bolts.

32   Lubricate the Cylinder Walls

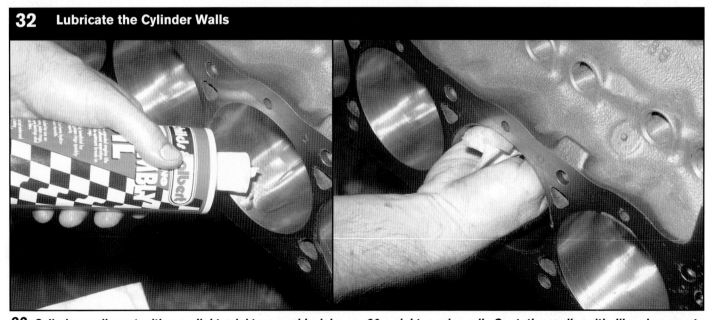

32–Cylinder walls get either a lightweight assembly lube or 30-weight engine oil. Coat the walls with liberal amounts of lubrication.

33 Cover Your Rod Bolts

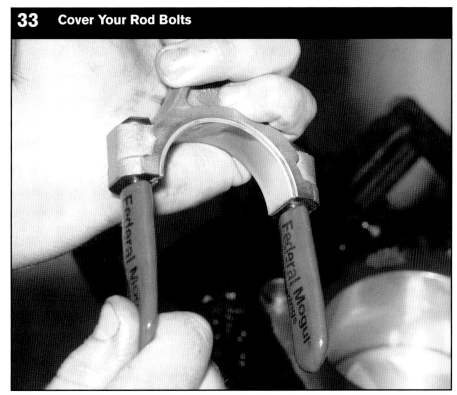

33–Since you don't want to nick cylinder walls or crankshaft journals, the rod bolts need to be covered with some sort of protection. Rod-bolt condoms prevent cylinder wall or crank journal nickage. Damage the crankshaft journal or cylinder wall and you can expect unnecessary time and expense machining out the damage.

34 Install the Pistons & Rods

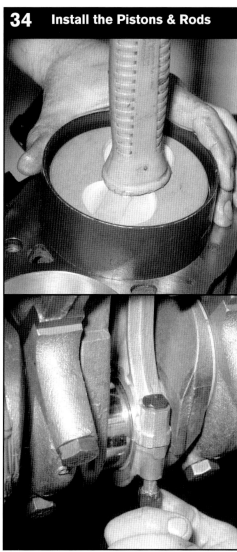

34–Piston-ring compressors vary in design. Seasoned builders use billet compressors that are bore-size specific, but adjustable ring compressors are cheap, easy to use, and perfect for the hobbyist. With the piston in the bore, guide the rod to the journal and carefully seat it in place. Hand-snug the rod nuts.

TORQUING FASTENERS

35 Torque the Rod Bolts

35–Torque 5/16-inch rod bolts to 19 to 24 ft-lbs. When you are working with 3/8-inch rod bolts, torque them to 40 to 45 ft-lbs. Remember to use lubrication on these bolts prior to torquing.

MASTER MECHANIC TIP

36 Degree the Cam

PRO TIP *35—It's time to degree the short block. We degree an engine because we want to determine both valve and piston timing events. Using the information provided by the cam card, we determine valve timing events by running the crankshaft two full revolutions. With a top-dead-center indicator (a dial indicator), we determine true piston location. This helps us determine compression height.*

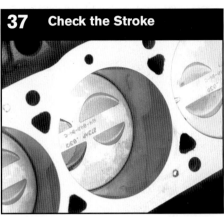

37 Check the Stroke

37—With the pistons and rods installed, we can confirm the 289's short 2.87-inch stroke. The 302 has a 3.00-inch stroke. The taller-deck 351W and 351C have a 3.50-inch stroke.

THE REST OF THE BOTTOM END

With our bottom end together, camshaft installed, tolerances checked, and camshaft degreed, we're ready to button up the short block. Before you begin installing the timing set and oil pan, it's a good idea to go back and double-check everything. Check crankshaft end-play, connecting rod side clearances, piston deck height on all bores, and the torque settings on all the bolts. Check the main cap bolt and connecting rod bolt torque readings. This consumes a bit more time, but it gives you peace of mind, knowing everything is tight and fitted together properly.

Timing covers tend to be a point of confusion for Ford buffs because there are so many different types. Early 1962 to '67 221/260/289-ci small-blocks have a common timing cover that has the timing pointer cast into the cover. These are pretty easy to identify. It gets tricky if you try to use one of these covers with a later-model harmonic balancer. We suggest sticking with a period balancer whenever you use this timing cover. Use a late-model balancer with this cover and you won't be able to see the timing marks with a timing light.

Beginning in 1968, Ford went to the bolt-on timing pointer in the same location as the cast-in pointer. With this change came a change in the harmonic balancer markings as well. Keep these changes in mind when you are buying a timing cover. This balancer/cover combo stayed consistent until the 1980s.

When Ford went to Central Fuel Injection (CFI) and Sequential Electronic Fuel Injection (SEFI) in the 1980s, the timing cover and harmonic balancer changed as a result. With this change came a cast-in pointer for magnetic pick-up timing lights on the right-hand side of the engine instead of the left.

Another point of confusion with timing covers is crankshaft oil seals. There are two types of seals – one with a lip (which presses in from the front) and one without a lip (which presses in from the inside against a lip in the timing cover). It's real easy to get this mixed up and install the wrong seal in the wrong cover. Don't make this mistake or you will have oil leaks.

Yet another area that confuses enthusiasts is the oil slinger that slides on the crankshaft. The only time we ever have to concern ourselves with this slinger is when we're using a dual-roller timing set. The oil slinger becomes too wide for the application, rubbing up against the timing chain. This is why we have to flatten out the oil slinger whenever we run a dual-roller timing set. Check this clearance carefully before the timing cover is installed. Also check clearances at the timing cover itself. Sometimes, this oil slinger can get into the oil seal, causing the same kind of problem.

Since we deal with a world of aftermarket components that don't always fit together well, we have to check everything for proper clearance when it is installed. One example is the oil pump and pick-up. Not all oil pumps clear the crankshaft counterweight. This involves some grinding of the oil pump housing prior to installation. Use a heavy-duty oil pump shaft, even when you are building a stock engine. Stock oil pump shafts can shear, causing a total loss of oil pressure and the risk of engine failure. Spend the money on a heavy-duty shaft in the interest of engine safety.

When it's time to install the pick-up and pan, check pick-up-to-pan clearances before installing the pan. You want the pick-up within 1/2 inch of the bottom of the pan. But, you don't want it touching the pan. Use a wad of modeling clay between the pick-up and pan to determine clearance.

There are two basic kinds of oil pan gaskets available for small-block Fords. There's the one-piece pan gasket we see a lot on the 5.0L High Output small-blocks. This is an outstanding piece because it minimizes the chances of oil leakage. If you're an old die-hard for vintage methods, go for the four-piece pan gasket and some good old-fashioned horse sense. The side rail gaskets get a modest dressing of silicone sealer between the gasket and block pan rail. There is no real need for sealer between the gasket and pan, but the choice is yours. With the rubber end gaskets in place, you need a small glob of silicone sealer where the side rail gaskets touch the end gaskets. This closes up any gaps where the four gaskets meet.

Assemble the Rest of the Bottom End

1 Crankshaft Oil Seal

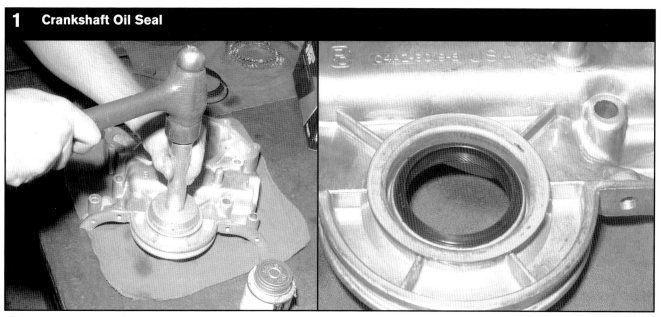

1–Timing cover installation begins with the crankshaft oil seal. There are two types. The seal shown here installs from the outside and has a lip. The other type doesn't have a lip and installs from the inside. In any case, the seal's inner lip should be lubricated and laid against the crank from the inside out to ensure a good seal.

2 Silicone Sealer

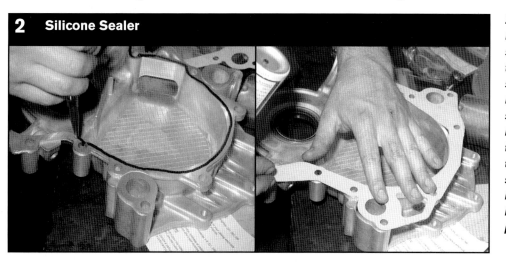

2–Timing cover gasket installation begins with silicone sealer as shown. Resist the temptation to slap on tons of sealer. Use a super-thin bead like this one. This allows the sealer to do its job without being squeezed out all over the place. Although we haven't trimmed the gasket here, we suggested doing so in the interest of a clean job. Gaskets hanging out all over the place look unsightly.

3 Install the Timing Cover

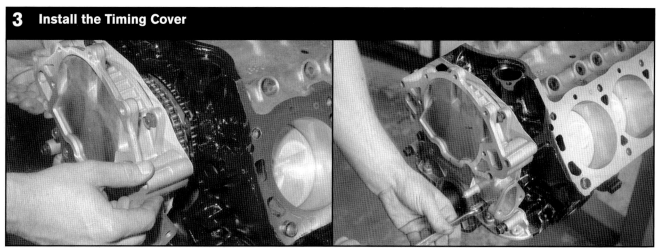

3–Timing cover installation is critical because we want the cover centered right where it's supposed to go. This means it needs to be centered on the crankshaft (using the harmonic balancer as a guide) and on the bolts.

4 Install the Balancer

4–The new harmonic balancer from Mustangs Etc. is lubricated with engine assembly lube. Did you remember to lubricate the seal?

5 Find the TDC

5–A closer look at the Mustangs Etc. harmonic balancer shows a greater array of timing marks that the factory didn't give us. Right now, we're at TDC on cylinder number 1, ready for distributor installation.

THE TOP END

With our short-block buttoned up and ready for combustion, it's time to approach the cylinder head and induction system. While this may seem like a simple segment of engine assembly, it's so easy to screw it up. All deck surfaces must be clean and free of imperfections. It's a good idea to do a dry run with the cylinder heads and valvetrain, especially if you are running a high-lift camshaft. A dry-run includes bolting on the cylinder heads without the head gaskets and installing the valvetrain to check valve-to-piston clearances.

Checking valve-to-piston clearances involves placing a wad of modeling clay in the piston valve reliefs, bolting the head and valvetrain in place, and hand-cranking the engine two revolutions. Remove the cylinder head and see how deep the valve impressions are in the clay. You need at least .050 inch of clearance between the valve and piston. If you are running a high-lift camshaft and don't perform this check, you risk valve-to-piston contact and severe engine damage. Even .050 inch clearance isn't enough when you are running a high-lift hydraulic camshaft. At high revs, the valves can float, closing this gap in short order.

When it's time to permanently install the cylinder heads, we suggest Fel-Pro's Print-O-Seal head gaskets, which provide a solid seal around the cylinder bores and coolant passages. When you are laying each head gasket in place, observe the coolant passages. Are they at the rear of the block? Each head gasket has passages at one end of the gasket. These coolant passages go at the rear of the block – always – with no exceptions. Installing the head gaskets backwards, with these passages at the front of the block, will cause overheating and serious engine damage. The word "FRONT" on these gaskets means exactly that – "FRONT."

Make sure you have clean cylinder head bolts and threads. Lubricate the cylinder head bolts with engine oil before installation. Torque the head bolts from the center out, torquing them in one-third values for uniform seating.

This ensures good cylinder head seating and sealing. When you are finished tightening the cylinder head bolts, recheck the torque again.

When you are installing the valvetrain, make sure all rocker arms have sufficient lubrication. Use engine assembly lube on the fulcrums and tips. Soak the lifters in engine oil, which fills them up with oil prior to engine start. This isn't a mandatory step, but it is a good idea when you're installing lifters.

With hydraulic lifters (flat-tappet and roller), adjust the rocker arms in time with the engine. Begin with number-1 cylinder and follow the firing order. Make sure you know the firing order. Most flat-tappet camshafts follow the old 221/260/289/302 firing order of 1-5-4-2-6-3-7-8. The roller cams go with the 351W firing order – which is 1-3-7-2-6-5-4-8. Make sure you know the correct firing order.

Hand-crank the engine and follow the firing order. As each intake valve seats fully, adjust the valve lash by cranking the adjustment down until the rocker arm touches the valvestem, and tighten clockwise 1/2 turn. If you expect to spin the engine high, go with 1/4 turn to minimize valve float.

If you are running a mechanical camshaft, valve clearances are typically .010 inch on both valves. See your camshaft manufacturer's instructions for specifics. Not all of them are .010 inch. Sometimes, the cam manufacturer wants you to check the valve lash with the engine hot. This is important to remember because parts grow as they heat up. Things expand, which changes clearances.

When it's time to bolt on the intake manifold, take extra care to remember proper sealing at the intake ports and cooling passages. This is an easy one to overlook in your haste for a completed engine. Use gasket shellac on the intake ports, just for extra measure. Silicone sealer works best around the cooling passages. Even though every gasket maker will provide you with end-rail gaskets, toss them in the trash. Apply a large bead of silicone sealer along those rails. As the sealer cures, it closes those gaps completely, providing a perfect seal, keeping the oil inside.

Assemble the Top End

1 Install the Head Gaskets

1–Fel-Pro from Federal-Mogul is our gasket of choice. Installing the cylinder head gaskets is very critical because you can install these gaskets backwards. "FRONT" means FRONT with small-block Ford head gaskets. Coolant passages must be positioned at the rear of the block for proper coolant flow. We suggest Fel-Pro Print-O-Seal head gaskets for best results.

2 Install the Heads

2–Cylinder heads are installed next. Make sure the block dowels are installed first.

MASTER MECHANIC TIP PRO TIP

3 Calibrate the Torque Wrench

3–Proper torque-wrench use is something we tend to overlook in our haste for a finished engine. First, never remove bolts with a torque wrench. Secondly, always zero the torque wrench after use. Following these rules helps keep your torque wrench calibrated.

TORQUING FASTENERS

4 Torque the Head Bolts

4–Cylinder-head bolts are torqued in third values from the inside out. Begin at the two center head bolts and torque them to 50 ft-lbs, working your way outward to the ends of the head. Next, torque the head bolts to 60 ft-lbs. Final torque is 65 to 72 ft-lbs. Double-check your torque readings.

5   Lubricate the Lifter Bores

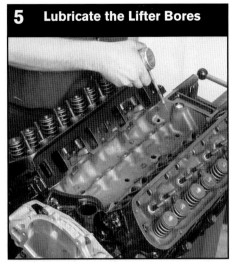

5–Engine oil is applied to the lifter bores to ensure smooth installation and initial operation.

6   Install the Lifters

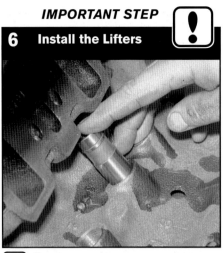

! 6–We're using a flat-tappet hydraulic camshaft from Crane Cams. Lifter faces get a dressing of cam lube, then they're installed as shown.

7   Install the Pushrods

7–Pushrods are next. Lubricate each end of the pushrod with engine assembly lube for best results.

8   Install the Rocker Arms

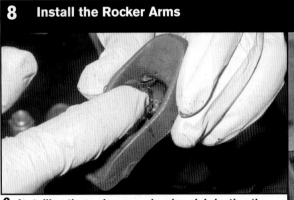

8–Installing the rocker arms involves lubricating the fulcrum with engine assembly lube and positioning the rocker in place. Check the rocker-arm-to-valvestem relationship. The rocker needs to be centered squarely on the valvestem.

9   Use Poly-Locs

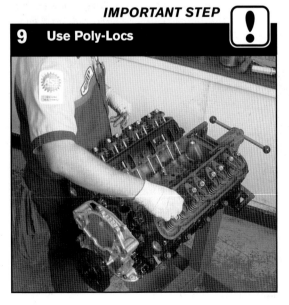

! 9–We learned something valuable with the screw-in rocker-arm studs that we installed during cylinder head build-up. Whenever you use stock rocker-arm lock nuts, you risk backing the screw-in studs out. If you do this, we suggest the use of aftermarket Poly-Loc rocker-arm nuts, which won't cause the stud to back out.

10   Adjust the Rocker Arms

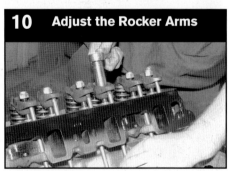

10–Rocker-arm adjustment consists of running the rocker-arm nut down to where the rocker arm touches the valvestem, then giving it 1/2 turn. If you're going to spin it high, give it 1/4 turn to allow for valve float. Small-blocks with mechanical lifters get .010-inch clearance on both the intake and exhaust valves.

11 Install Gasket Ports

11–Intake manifold gaskets rarely get the right gasket sealer treatment. We're going to show you how to do it properly here. Intake ports get a thin application of regular old gasket shellac. If you are using Fel-Pro Print-O-Seal, leave the intake ports alone.

12 Intake Gasket Coolant Passages

12–Coolant passages get silicone sealer for extra added measure. This keeps coolant where it belongs.

13 Seat the Gaskets

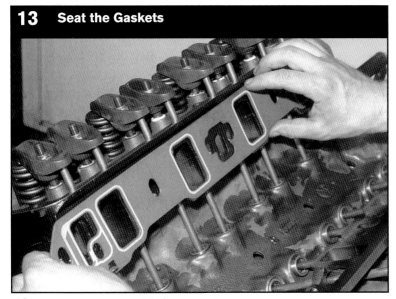

13–Intake manifold gaskets are seated in place, taking extra care to ensure proper sealing.

14 Trim Coolant Passages

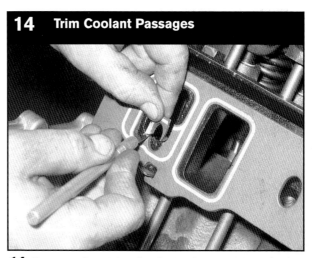

14–Yes – we forgot to trim the coolant passages for our vintage 289 small-block. These gaskets are actually designed around the 351W coolant passage. We cut the passages as shown for the 289 – hopefully you'll remember to do it before you start messing with the gasket sealer.

15 Clean the Intake Rails

15–Intake rails are cleaned with a strong solvent to ensure good sealer adhesion.

IMPORTANT STEP

16 Use Silicone Instead

16–*Gasket manufacturers all provide intake manifold end gaskets. However, we discourage their use. A bead of silicone gasket sealer works very well in preventing oil leakage. When the sealer cures, it expands, forming a tight seal along the ends of the intake manifold.*

17 Seat the Manifold

17–*The factory cast-iron four-barrel intake manifold is installed, setting it down carefully to ensure proper port and bolt-hole alignment.*

TORQUING FASTENERS

18 Torque Down the Manifold

18–*The intake manifold is torqued in crisscross fashion from one side to the other. Torque in third values, just like the cylinder heads. Begin with 15 ft-lbs, then 20, and then 22 ft-lbs. Check your torque readings on all bolts.*

19 Clean the Mounting Surface

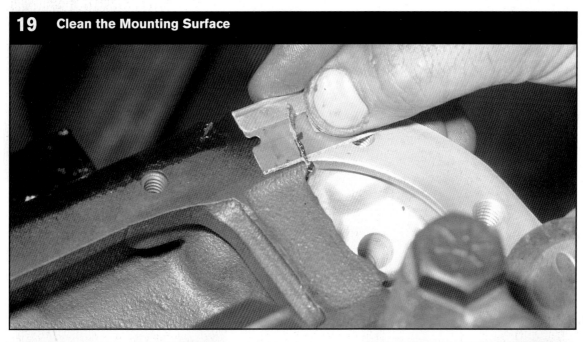

19–*Roll the engine over and prepare for oil pan installation. First, clean up gasket mating surfaces with a razor blade as shown.*

20 Install the Oil Pump

20–*Oil pump installation is handled first by putting the shaft in place and then installing the pump. Install the gasket between the pump and block. Then, Loctite the bolts. Make sure the crankshaft counterweight clears the pump.*

21 Check the Clearance

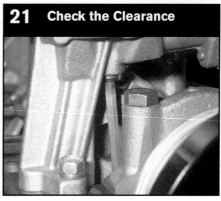

21–*Close inspection of the oil pump and driveshaft is important to ensuring proper crankshaft-counterweight-to-pump clearance.*

22   Install the Oil Pan Gasket

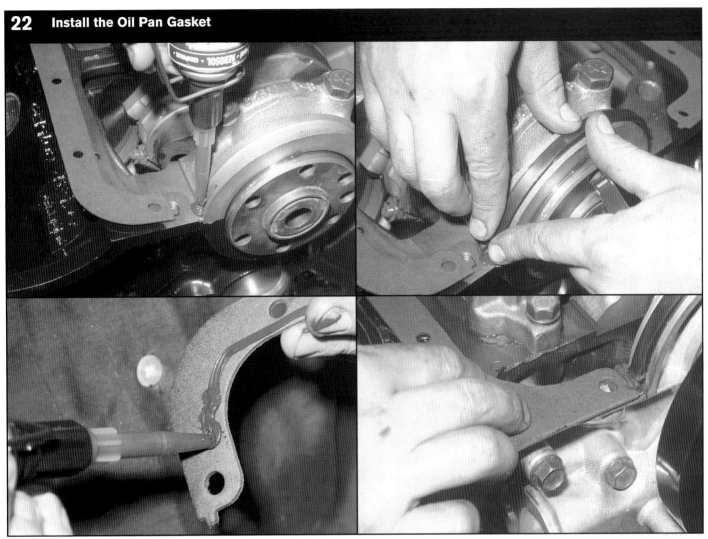

22–Oil pan gasket installation begins with silicone sealer at the unions located at both ends of the pan. Rubber end gaskets are installed first, taking care to seat them firmly in the timing cover and rear main cap. Use silicone sealer between the gasket and pan rails. There is no need to use sealer between the pan and gasket. There is also a one-piece pan gasket available from Fel-Pro.

23   Seat the Pan

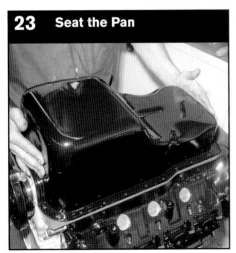

23–This reproduction steel oil pan from Virginia Classic Mustang is a perfect fit. The pan is seated in place, making sure all gasket segments remain in place.

24   Hand-Tighten the Bolts

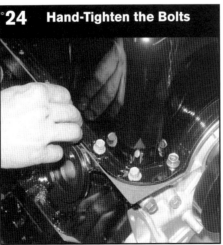

24–We have secured an AMK Engine Fastener Kit from Virginia Classic Mustang. These oil-pan bolts are hand tightened while the silicone sealer is soft and pliable.

TORQUING FASTENERS

25   Torque the Bolts

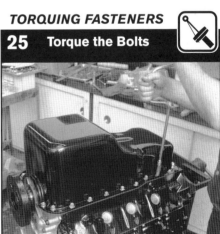

25–Oil pan boils are run down with a speed handle prior to torquing. Tighten bolts in a crisscross fashion back and forth across the pan to 9 to 11 ft-lbs. After a sit period, check the torque again.

26 Install the Valvecover Gaskets

26–Period-style Cobra valvecovers from Virginia Classic Mustang are installed next. Use gasket sealer between the gasket and valvecover.

27 Install the Valvecovers

27–Finally, seat the valvecovers and tighten them down. There is no need for sealer between the gasket and cylinder head.

28 Install the Carburetor

28–We're going with original equipment on this relatively stock 289. This is the 480-cfm Autolite 4100 carburetor for the 289-4V engine, rebuilt and precision tuned by Pony Carburetors. You can step up to a 600-cfm version of this carburetor and gain more horsepower and torque.

Did You Know?

WORKBENCH TIP

Earlier in this chapter, we told you about proper cylinder-head-gasket installation. Coolant passages always go at the back of the block. But, what if you've already installed the cylinder heads and aren't sure you installed the cylinder head gaskets properly? Look at the front of the block on both sides where the cylinder head and block meet. If you see the head gasket, it's installed properly. If you don't see the head gasket, it's installed backwards.

A quick way to check for proper head-gasket installation is to look for the head gasket in each front corner of the block. If the head gasket isn't visible, the gasket is installed backwards.

CHAPTER 6

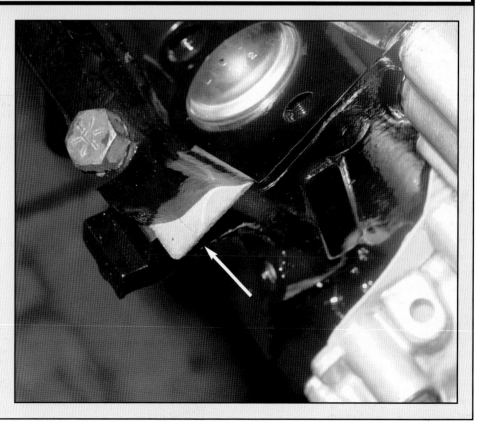

BREAK-IN AND TUNING

Few things are as religious as firing a new engine for the first time. With those first hot pulses of reciprocation, a new engine begins to warm up and come into its own. But, before you can fire the engine safely, you need to make sure the engine and all of its support systems are ready for action. Does the engine have a good cooling system? What about the exhaust system? Are the catalytic converters in good condition? Have you examined the ignition and fuel systems? What about the car's electrical system? What kind of shape is the driveline in? Is the driveline up to the amount of power you intend to throw at it? What about the braking system? Have you looked at the tires lately?

We ask these questions because your vehicle needs to be a complete, well-functioning package when you go to take that first spin with a new engine. Building a powerful engine and installing it in a vehicle with really bad brakes is just plain stupid. Putting a clogged radiator with rotted hoses in front of a new engine is courting trouble. How good is your vehicle infrastructure?

COOLING SYSTEM

It goes without saying that your new engine needs a good support system

Did You Burp It?

WORKBENCH TIP

Fresh engines need coolant in contact with every square inch of the water jackets. When you are servicing the cooling system with the correct mix of antifreeze and water, keep the heater hose or temperature sender loose to allow all air to escape from the water jackets before firing the engine. Leaving a hose or a sender loose at the top of the engine allows air to escape, which eliminates all air pockets (hot spots) inside the engine.

While we have your attention, use the right mix of antifreeze and water. When you use too much antifreeze, you hurt the coolant's ability to transfer heat from the engine to the radiator. Too much antifreeze can be worse than having too little.

to live a long time. Start with a brand new radiator and a cooling system filter in the upper radiator hose. The coolant filter captures stray rust particles that dislodge and wind up trapped in new radiator tubes. During the first several thousand miles, check the coolant filter and make sure it is clean. A clogged coolant filter will create the same kind of overheating issues a clogged radiator will.

You would be surprised how many of us will install the old thermostat in a new engine to save a few bucks. But, here are the facts about thermostats. First fact, *never* run your engine without a thermo-stat. Simpleton shop logic believes not running a thermostat will help the engine run cooler. Perhaps it might in northern Canada, but not in Missouri in the middle of the summer. When you remove the thermostat, the coolant never has a chance to stay in the radiator long enough to get rid of its heat. As coolant rushes through the engine and radiator, it just gets hotter and hotter, causing your engine to over-heat. If you get stuck in traffic without a thermostat, count on a boil over. Cruise down the highway on a hot day without a thermostat and you will experience a boil over. The thermostat is very necessary to proper engine cooling.

It's a good idea to stick with a 180-degree thermostat for a good balance of heat transfer and heat retention. Hot-rodders like to run 160-degree thermostats mostly because it has become habit. Small radiators, which are common in hot rods, don't get rid of heat as efficiently as large ones, hence the logic behind a cooler thermostat. But, 160-degree thermostats aren't always the answer to cool cruising. When we speak of heat retention, this is just as important as heat dissipation. Engines have a minimum temperature that they have to function at – especially computer-controlled engines, which have to run at 192 degrees. A good rule of thumb is this : older carbureted engines need 180-degree thermostats. Newer, computer-controlled engines need 192- to 195-degree thermostats. Proper engine temperature is important to proper fuel atomization and burning. It's also important to good oil flow throughout the engine. The happiest engines run with a coolant temperature of 180 to 200 degrees Fahrenheit.

Complement your new radiator with all new cooling system hoses and a new water pump. Even though a water pump may look fine and be free of leaks, that doesn't mean it was pumping effectively when the old engine came out. Water pump impellers become covered with rust and scale, which reduces pumping efficiency. When you're shopping for a new water pump, aim for a high-flow unit in the best interest of cooling efficiency.

When you fill the cooling system the first time, opt for the appropriate 50/50 mix of ethylene-glycol and water. A lot of us fill the cooling system with water, which really isn't a good idea. If you're concerned with leaks, then be mindful of this when you are assembling the engine. Do it right and avoid the leak fest when it's time to fire the engine. Double-check all hoses and connections before the coolant goes in. Use a good cooling system rust inhibitor while you're pouring in the coolant. Because coolant grows with temperature, don't fill the radiator to the top. Fill it just to the top of the tubes. As the engine warms up, the coolant will expand and take up the top tank. Have a pan ready to catch any overflow.

READY TO LAUNCH

When you are about to fire a new engine, there are important considerations you must be attentive to first. For the break-in period, it's a good idea to use Castrol conventional SAE 30 oil – save the synthetic for after the engine is

Since Jim Grubbs wanted to know the kind of power a stock small-block Ford makes, he wasn't releasing the 289 to Jeff Fischbach until it was fired and had a couple of dyno pulls under its belt for Mustang Monthly magazine.

broken in. Although a good many of us never do this, you should prime the oiling system and be sure there's oil pressure. This not only confirms oil pressure and flow, it pre-lubes the bearings for that initial fire-up. Oiling system primers fit into the distributor opening and onto the oil pump shaft. When you spin the oil pump (the drill needs to be running in reverse, or counterclockwise), oil should flow from the rocker arms and there should be a healthy reading at the oil pressure gauge.

When you install the distributor, make sure you get the timing right. Put that timing mark on TDC (number-1 cylinder) and put the rotor on number 1. Installing small-block Ford distributors is a pain in the neck. It's hard to get

Jeff's stock 289-4V engine is on the dyno and ready for action. Jim Grubbs' talented staff has done a magnificent job on this engine. It is built for good low-end torque and solid reliability. We're about to learn how much power it makes.

the distributor seated and timed properly. A good rule of thumb is to get the rotor as close to number 1 as possible, then hand-crank the engine, which gets the distributor lined up with the oil pump shaft. Finally, back-crank the engine and see where the rotor is positioned.

Carburetor static tuning is pretty simple. Be it an Autolite or a Holley, the drill is the same. Idle mixture screws get seated, then backed out 1-1/2 turns. Idle speed tends to be hit and miss. It's a good idea to back the idle speed screw off to where the throttle plates are closed, then milk the speed screw open (during cranking) until the engine fires.

After you've broken in the cam, let the engine run at a fast idle (about 1,200 rpm) until the thermostat opens. Keep the radiator cap in place, but loosen it enough to allow air to escape without spraying you with coolant. Like we said earlier, fill the radiator only to the top of the tubes, but no further until the engine is hot and the coolant fully expands. It's also important to remember coolant has a higher boiling point

Mustang Monthly *magazine wanted to run stock exhaust manifolds on this engine for accurate horsepower and torque readings. Unfortunately, Jim Grubbs Motorsports didn't have the necessary exhaust plumbing to run stock manifolds. As a result, Andy is bolting on a set of dyno headers for this one. The engine made 212 hp and 282 ft-lbs of torque.*

MASTER MECHANIC TIP PRO TIP

PRO TIP *Ignition timing is set two ways. At idle, timing should be dialed in around 12 degree BTDC. Total advance should be no higher than 36 degrees BTDC. During our dyno pull, Jim Grubbs was able to get the maximum amount of horsepower and torque at 34 degrees BTDC.*

under pressure. Keep the radiator cap secured once all air has escaped from the water jackets. You may actually burp off all air by removing the heater hose at the intake manifold as the radiator is being filled. This allows most of the air to escape without having to wait for an open thermostat.

If you are running a flat-tappet camshaft like we are, the engine must run at 2,500 rpm for 20 to 30 minutes to work-harden the cam lobes and set the wear pattern on the lifters. When we fired our Jim Grubbs 289, it sat on the dyno and roared with authority for 20 minutes to properly wear in the cam

lobes. You don't have to do this with a roller camshaft.

While you're wearing in the camshaft, check the ignition timing and set it to approximately 12 degrees BTDC at idle. Watch the exhaust headers/manifolds for excessive heat (glowing), which can mean late timing or a lean fuel mixture. Both can

MASTER MECHANIC TIP PRO TIP

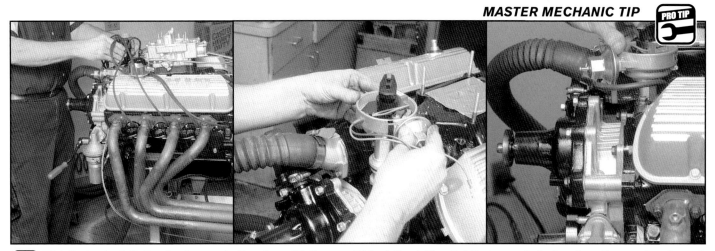

PRO TIP *Distributor installation is always challenging with the small-block Ford. The distributor seats just so far – then we hand-crank the engine backwards and wait for the distributor to seat. Then, we check the rotor indexing for proper position.*

permanently damage the engine. A lean mixture can mean jets that are too small. It can also mean the fuel line is too small for how much power the engine is making. What size is your Ford's fuel line? Most of them are 5/16 inch, which is too small for a powerful V-8. We suggest the use of a 3/8-inch fuel line if horsepower rises above 300. When power rises above 400, you need a 7/16-inch fuel line.

When the engine has both reached operating temperature and run long enough to break in the camshaft (flat-tappet only), it's time to set total ignition timing. Rev the engine to 3,500 rpm and hold it there. Check the timing and determine how many degrees you have at the pointer. Total advance should be in at 3,500 rpm. Each and every engine is different based on what it has for a camshaft, cylinder heads, and induction. Our project 289 engine was all finished at 34 degrees BTDC at 3,500 rpm. Some engines can go as far as 41 degrees

BTDC, but this is discouraged. You have to develop a feel for your engine in all of this tuning. With the engine at 3,500 rpm, slowly move the distributor toward advance until it begins to misfire. If everything is pretty typical, it will get smoother as you move total timing toward 36 degrees BTDC. When you creep past 36 degrees, it should begin to run rough. Bring the timing back a pinch to 34 to 36 degrees BTDC. That's optimum timing.

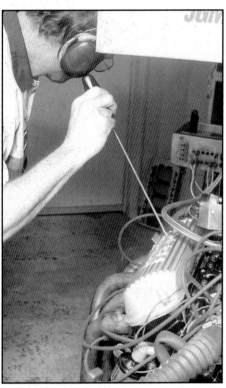

Jim listens for unusual valvetrain noises during warm-up.

An empty engine bay is like the artist's canvas – ready for our close attention. Before the 289 engine goes into this one, it's going to get spruced up.

Gunk engine cleaner is the same great solvent we were using 35 years ago to debunk engine compartments. It still works very well on the gummiest of engine bays. We spray it on, let it soak in, and then hose it off. Lots of sanding, too!

The Jim Grubbs 289 receives its Center-force Dual-Friction clutch on the tailgate of a pick-up truck.

Classic Krylon semi-flat black looks great on a classic Mustang engine compartment. This is the most perfect paint and color. It goes right on and dries quickly.

Our 289 is ready to go to work. We have remembered important issues, such as a new radiator, engine mounts, clutch, throwout bearing, water pump, and any other potential weak spots.

High-Performance Pulleys

WORKBENCH TIP

PERFORMANCE TIP

Before you go any further with your engine, how high do you expect to spin it? High-revving engines need proper pulley sizing. Underdrive pulleys (not shown here) reduce the speed of accessories like the alternator, water pump, and power-steering pump. So do extra-large accessory pulleys like this one from MCE Engines. The large alternator pulley keeps the engine from blowing the alternator windings.

This is a standard pulley package, with smaller alternator and water pump pulleys.

The Fuel System

This is a typical 5/16-inch fuel line on a 302-ci Ford. If you're going to pump up the power, this won't be enough.

Fuel-line size is critical to performance and safe operation. Most factory fuel lines are 5/16 inch, not enough for engines over 300 horsepower. Most need 3/8-inch lines. When power rises above 400, you need 7/16 inch.

Engines that make over 400 horsepower need 7/16-inch fuel lines, like this powerhouse from MCE Engines. You can have the strongest fuel pump in the world, but if you don't have enough fuel line to feed it, your engine will be starved.

The Fuel System (continued)

WORKBENCH TIP

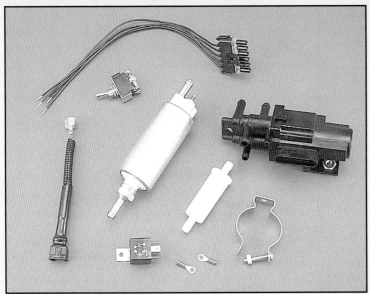

Fuel-injected small-blocks need the same kind of consideration as carbureted engines. You need a fuel pump, injectors, and a pressure regulator that will keep up with the demands of a high-horse small-block.

Fuel-injected small-blocks also have this part to think about: the fuel-pressure regulator. We like adjustable regulators ourselves, which give you control over fuel pressure.

Fuel injectors are sized in pounds-per-hour rates. Stock is typically 19 lbs/hr.

The Exhaust System

PERFORMANCE TIP

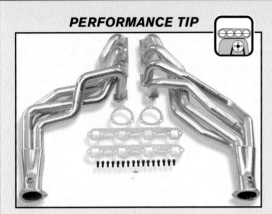

Choosing the right exhaust system is as important as choosing the right sized carburetor or radiator. It becomes a decision you will have to live with. Header selection boils down to budget and how you'll use the vehicle. Short-tube headers radiate less heat and interfere less than long-tube headers, but they don't build as much power. Ceramic headers cost more, but they contain heat, which keeps the engine compartment (and the cabin!) cooler. Don't fire a fresh engine with any less than a good exhaust system and the right headers. Crushed and damaged header tubes hold in combustion heat, which makes the affected cylinders run much hotter and could cause permanent engine damage.

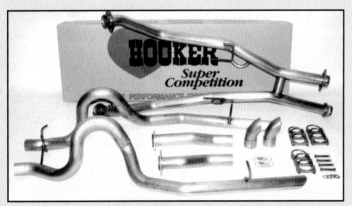

When you are shopping for headers, don't forget the rest of your exhaust system. Loose muffler bafflers and dented and crushed pipes will hurt performance. They can also cause engine damage by containing excessive heat that should go out the tailpipe.

Late-model Fords with catalytic converters need a second look when it comes to exhaust system integrity. Clogged catalytic converters will cause excessive exhaust-system temperatures. This takes an incredible toll on a new engine. Replace the cats with free-breathing, high-performance converters.

IMPORTANT STEP

Computer-controlled, late-model Fords need close inspection to make sure all the sensors are in proper working order. Without them, computer-controlled engines flounder badly. Faulty sensors can cause serious irregularities in fuel and spark curves, which can damage the engine.

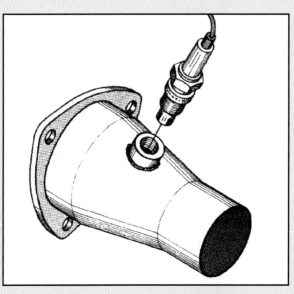

Typically some of the weakest links in computer-controlled Fords are the oxygen sensors. These sensors determine fuel mixture.

MASTER MECHANIC TIP

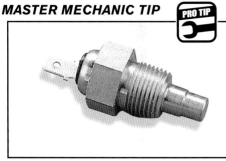

PRO TIP *Senders are something we never think about enough. Coolant temperature and oil pressure senders need to be fresh and accurate. Not knowing these vital signs can cost you plenty.*

Dialing in the vacuum advance is an art. You want the vacuum advance to work hand in hand with the mechanical advance. As the throttle is opened, the vacuum advance should deliver a soft spike advance in the timing, which segues into the mechanical advance as revs increase. The vacuum advance's job is to give an initial spark advance spike when the throttle is opened. The trick is to adjust it to where it's a smooth transition from vacuum to mechanical advance. The result is a smooth application of torque as RPM increases. If you get pinging

IMPORTANT STEP

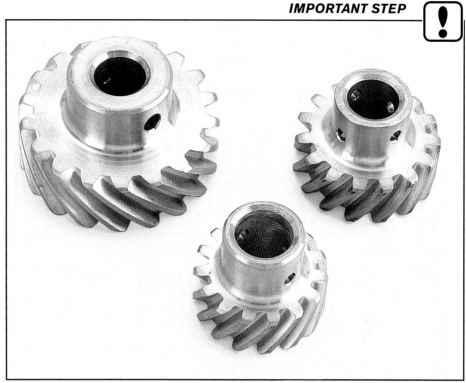

! *Before you spin the engine, what kind of camshaft are you running? Roller camshafts need steel distributor gears. Iron gears should only be used with flat-tappet camshafts.*

(spark knock) coming off idle, you need to slow the rate of vacuum advance. If the engine tends to fall on

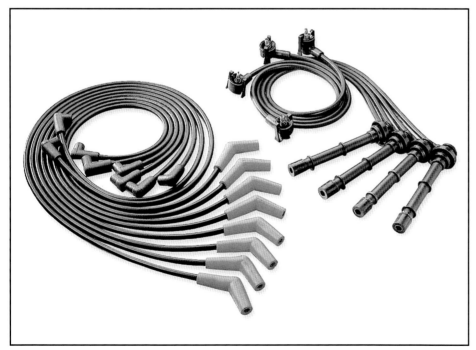

We don't give much thought to ignition wiring, but it can cause engine damage via crossfire and misfire. This is especially critical if you are running nitrous or a supercharger.

its face, you need to quicken the rate of vacuum advance coming off idle.

Once the engine has had a chance to get hot and be driven, it's a good idea to examine the coolant for discoloring, check the oil (which should be dark or black to some degree from assembly lube and molybdenum cam grease), and check for leaks. The rear main seal area should be free of leakage. Closely inspect around the freeze plugs, intake manifold gaskets, valve-cover gaskets, and the front timing cover.

When you have 500 to 1,000 miles on the engine, change the oil and run Mobil 1 10W30 synthetic engine oil with a Wix or Motorcraft oil filter. After you have 1,000 miles on the engine, do another inspection. Pull the dipstick and look at the oil. It should be free of debris and be relatively clear. If it is milky and looks like turkey gravy, you have coolant in the oil. The cause of coolant leakage must be determined and corrected immediately. If it is a heavy gravy, like mud in consistency, the engine must be torn down and inspected. Too much coolant in the oil will damage the bearings and rings, rendering a new engine old in short order. When you remember how important that layer of oil between moving parts is to engine survival, having pure oil in the pan becomes paramount.

It's also a good idea to do a spark plug reading. The plugs should have a nice tan glow – not black and sooty, and certainly not snow white. Black and sooty means a rich fuel mixture. Snow white means it's running too lean. Snow white with dots of aluminum is cause for alarm – too lean with piston melt. Spark plugs that are oily means piston ring leakage or valveg-

uides that are in trouble. Rarely will you see oil on all eight spark plugs unless there was a gross error in assembly across eight bores.

While you are under the hood, listen to the engine at idle. Do any noises stand out? Any knocking or clicking? Do these noises happen cold or hot? Use a long-handled screwdriver to listen for noise and location. A steady clicking may be nothing more than the need for valve-lash adjustment. But, check the source of the noise immediately. Remove the valve covers and watch the valvetrain at idle. Ascertain the source of the clicking.

If there is a knock, especially down low in the engine, this is a reason to be more concerned about assembly issues, clearances, and the like. If there is a knock in rhythm with the crankshaft, remove spark plug wires one at a time and listen closely. If the knock goes away on a particular bore, the problem is serious and mandates a teardown. If a knock is in rhythm with combustion pulses and vanishes when you remove a spark plug wire, the same logic applies. You will have to knock the engine down and determine the cause.

Should You Run Synthetic?

WORKBENCH TIP

Priming the oiling system with a drill bathes the bearings in oil prior to engine start. Run the drill counterclockwise and watch for the flow of oil at the rocker arms. Observe oil pressure at the gauge as well if equipped.

There's a lot of debate over what kind of oil to use on a new engine. We suggest break-in with conventional 30-weight engine oil for the first 500 to 1,000 miles. Then, always use Mobil 1 10W30 synthetic engine oil. Based on millions of miles of reliable, wear-free use, there is no better engine oil for your small-block.

There has been a lot of debate through the years about the use of synthetic engine oil. During the initial fire-up and break-in period, we suggest the use of Castrol 30W or 10W30 weight engine oil with a Motorcraft oil filter. Run this oil for the first 500 to 1,000 miles, and then fill the pan with Mobil 1 10W30 weight engine oil along with a new fil-

ter. Some engine builders are comfortable with the use of synthetic engine oil during break-in. Because proper ring seating is so important to the longevity of an engine, we suggest going old school on this one – use regular 30W or 10W30 weight oil during break-in, then synthetic for the life of the engine.

CHAPTER 7

PERFORMANCE BUYER'S GUIDE

We're going to wrap this book up with a smattering of parts, accessories, and tools that make nice contributions to an engine-building project. Not all of them will be applicable to your engine-building project. Sometimes, it's nice to dream when we are planning our engines. It's nice to know what's out there. Whether you are building a budget small-block or a powerful engine for the track, the aftermarket offers a world of options designed to make your project a smashing success.

MASTER MECHANIC TIP

PRO TIP *If you're going to build a lot of engines, this cam-degreeing kit from Lunati Cams is a nice complement to your tool and equipment arsenal. A degree wheel and pointer enable you to know valve and piston timing events in great detail. If you're building just one engine, we suggest renting one of these locally.*

PERFORMANCE TIP

MSD's Pro-Billet distributor is what you want when it's time to belly up to the big table. This is the world's first billet distributor. MSD concluded that making a distributor from one piece of billet aluminum ensured reliability under the toughest of conditions – and accuracy to within 0.001 inch! Because this is a magnetic-pick-up ignition, it is extremely accurate – every time.

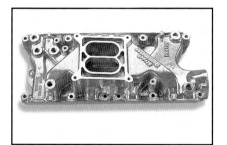

Holley's Street Dominator dual-plane intake manifold is the perfect manifold for mild engine builds where four-barrel carburetion and good low-end torque are important. This really isn't a high-rise manifold, but its long runners and low profile help your small-block make torque while keeping it all underneath the hood. You can even run a stock air cleaner on top of this manifold when you use the Holley 4160 (1850 series) carburetor.

MASTER MECHANIC TIP PRO TIP

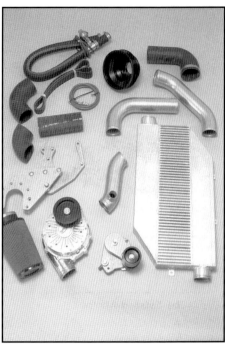

If you want to pump more power into your small-block Ford building without having to give up your first born, consider the purchase of a stroker kit from Scat Enterprises. Stroker kits range from simple, affordable nodular-iron cranks with I-beam rods to billet cranks with H-beam rods. Forged or hypereutectic pistons are also available. The choice is yours, depending on budget.

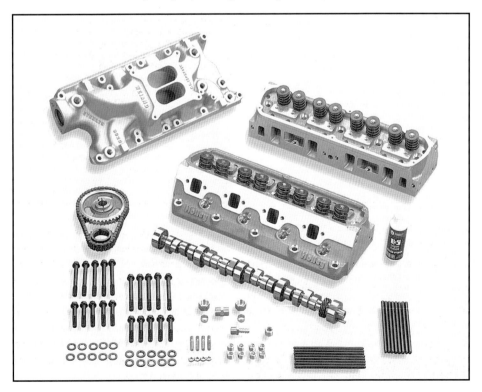

You can pick up some bonus bolt-on power from an ATI Procharger. Just look at this ATI Procharger intercooled centrifugal supercharger kit, scheduled for installation in Mustang Monthly magazine! ATI tells us this intercooled kit can add 50 to 85 percent more power to your small-block Ford, depending on how you build your engine. This burst of power comes from a great centrifugal design that is a proven industry standard, and the intercooler will cool down the intake charge, keeping things under control. Use this power responsibly and come out a winner.

Holley's SysteMax engine performance system for small-block Fords is available a couple of different ways for both carbureted and fuel-injected small-blocks. Shown here is the carbureted version, with a Weiand Stealth dual-plane intake manifold, Holley heads, a hot Lunati roller camshaft, and more! When you opt for the fuel-injected version, you get the fuel pump, larger throttle body and mass-air sensor, and a whole lot more! This is a nice package that works very well together.

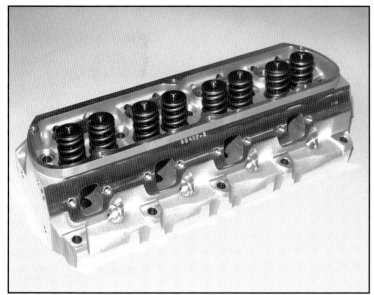
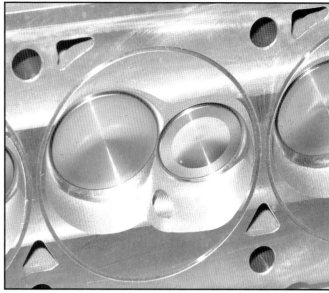

This is the Twisted Wedge cylinder head from Trick Flow Specialties. Meet one of the best aftermarket cylinder heads in the marketplace. It is 50-state smog legal – and it makes power! A 5.0L Cobra GT-40 engine with a set of these heads, GT-40 intake, Ford Racing E-303 camshaft, and stud-mounted rocker arms made 328 horsepower and 354 ft-lbs of torque. Not bad, considering it's all bolt-on performance. You'll need to research fitment issues with these because of their 2.02-inch intake valves. Make sure your piston-to-valve clearances will be within spec.

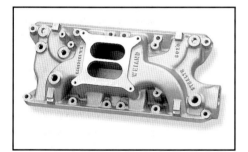

No matter what kind of street small-block you are building, a good broad torque curve is important at any power level. This is the Weiand Stealth dual-plane intake manifold from Holley. The Stealth is based on the good old-fashioned high-rise, dual-plane concept. However, its runner design enables your engine to make torque at both low and high RPM.

PERFORMANCE TIP

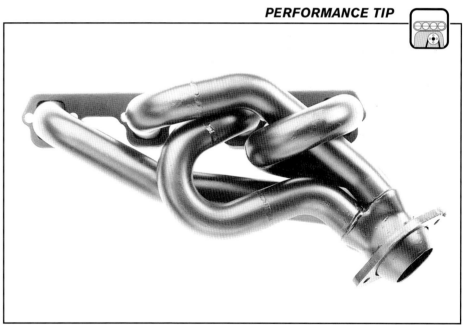

Pertronix has become legendary for its keen ability to design and engineer simple bolt-on products that make a big difference in performance. This is the new billet distributor from Pertronix, fitted with the Ignitor II ignition module. What this means for your small-block is simplicity. Static-time this distributor, fire the engine, and set the timing. That's all! It is factory-curved to perform right out of the box.

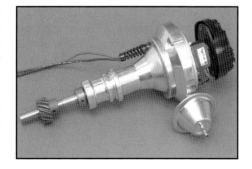

Throughout this book, we have addressed exhaust scavenging and the benefits thereof. Hooker Headers has been a key player in the exhaust scavenging game for more than 40 years. This is the Hooker Competition equal-length shorty header for late-model 5.0L Mustangs. The equal-length tubes mean improved performance due to uniform exhaust scavenging.

We don't think about fuel pumps much; that is, until it's time to fire the engine. Mustangs Etc. has your factory-original fuel pump for the small-block Ford. This fuel pump looks like the original rebuildable fuel pumps the small-block Fords had back in the 1960s, including the integral fuel filter that was so common then.

PERFORMANCE TIP

Nitrous oxide injection has long been a simple answer for quick horsepower. However, nitrous works successfully only when it is handled responsibly. NOS understands this and has a little something for everyone interested in quick, affordable, bolt-on power. NOS, once located in Southern Califfornana, is now a division of Holley Performance Products. There are whole nitrous-oxide systems available for carbureted and fuel-injected small-block Fords alike. Shop carefully and choose the best system for your application.

Regardless of what kind of fuel-injected small-block you build, you're going to need fuel injectors. Steeda has four basic kinds of fuel injectors available, depending on what you are building. The orange 19 lb/hr injector works in stock applications. Shown here are 24 lb/hr injectors (blue) for warmed-up street applications. What flow you choose depends on how much power your small-block is expected to make. This is especially critical with nitrous and supercharged applications where generous fuel-flow is important. Ask Steeda about the right injector for your injected small-block.

Small-block Fords have long been credited with having good, strong connecting rods throughout their 45-year history. However, when you're going to throw nitrous or a supercharger at a small-block Ford, or you intend to road-race, it's time for something stronger. This Lunati Street/Race connecting rod is perfect for applications where you could go beyond the envelope of a stock connecting rod. This rod is 5.400 inches in length, is bushed at the small end, and has cap screws for solid reliability.

This is the Autolite 4100 carburetor from Pony Carburetors. If ever there was a solid substitute for the Holley 4160, this is it. What you get from the Autolite 4100 is reliability. It's the most maintenance free carburetor we have ever seen. Install it. Tune it. Set the idle. And forget it. This is simply a great carburetor.

Ignitioneering can take your Autolite or Motorcraft distributor (including all Durasparks) and rebuild it to better-than-new specifications. These folks completely tear down the distributor, replace all necessary parts, install oil-impregnated bushings, and tune the distributor to your application.

PERFORMANCE TIP

Nothing makes a small-block Ford happier than new AMK hardware from Virginia Classic Mustang. The AMK Engine Hardware Kit from Virginia Classic Mustang has everything you need to assemble a small-block Ford except for the cylinder head bolts – which are available separately. This new hardware screws your engine together with solid integrity. It also looks nice in a fresh engine compartment.

PERFORMANCE TIP

Carbureted small-block folks tend to feel left out of the supercharger game because so many supercharger kits are available for fuel-injected Mustangs. But Paxton never forgot about the carburetor. There has always been a supercharger kit available from Paxton for carbureted small-block Fords – in particular the 289 and 302. More recently, Paxton has come out with a Novi 1200 supercharger kit for the 351W small-block. These carbureted kits enclose the whole carburetor inside a pressurized box.

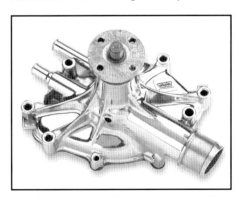

Anytime you can improve coolant flow through your small-block, you are extending its service life significantly. The Weiand Action-Plus water pump is a lightweight, highly polished piece for late-model, 5.0L fuel-injected Mustangs. It knocks 30 to 50 percent of the weight off the front of the engine. Inside, there's a premium quality bearing and seal for long life. This pump is designed for 1985 to '93 5.0L engines. There are also Action-Plus Weiand water pumps available for vintage small-block Fords.

We think of Trick Flow for some of the best cylinder heads in the marketplace, but did you know Trick Flow also does induction systems for carbureted and fuel-injected engines? Shown here is the 5.0L Street Intake for late-model small-block Fords. This is a natural complement for the Trick Flow heads mentioned earlier in this chapter.

ENGINE MATH

When you're building an engine, it's nice to be armed with the facts necessary to do it successfully. Much of engine building is about math — machining dimensions, compression and rod ratios, bore sizes, stroke, journal diameters, carburetors, port sizes, dynamic balancing, and all the rest of it. Without math, you cannot successfully build an engine. What follows are quick facts that will help you in your Ford engine building.

CUBIC-INCH DISPLACEMENT

Cubic-inch displacement is simply the volume displaced by the cylinders of your engine. So, if we calculate the volume of one cylinder, and multiply that figure times the number of cylinders, we have the engine's displacement.

The formula for a cylinder's volume is:

Pi x r² x S = Volume of one cylinder.

Where Pi is a mathematical constant equal to 3.14159, r is the radius of the cylinder, and S is the stroke. If you think back to your high school geometry, you may remember that a circle's radius is half the diameter. In this case, the diameter is equal to the bore (B), so *1/2B = r.* Plug that in, and our formula becomes:

Pi x (1/2B)² x S =
Volume of One Cylinder

We can simplify this further by plugging in the numerical value for Pi, then doing some basic algebra that doesn't necessarily need to be covered here — but trust us: the equation before is equal to this equation:

B x B x S x 0.7854 =
Volume of One Cylinder

To determine the engine's displacement, factor in the number of cylinders (N):

B x B x S x 0.7854 x N =
Engine displacement.

So, let's use this to figure out the displacement of a Ford engine that has a 4-inch Bore and a 3-inch Stroke:

4.000" x 4.000" x 3.00" x 0.7854 x 8 =
301.59 ci

Ford rounded 301.59 up to 302 ci, or 4.9L. (Note: One liter is equal to about 61 cubic inches.)

CALCULATING COMPRESSION RATIO

An engine's compression ratio is the ratio between two volumes: The volume of the cylinder and combustion chamber when the piston is at BDC, and the volume of the combustion chamber when the piston is at TDC. But there's more to consider than just cylinder volume and head cc's. To get the engine's TRUE compression ratio, you need to know these volumes:

- Combustion Chamber Volume (**C**)
- Compressed Head Gasket Volume (**G**)
- Piston/Deck Height (**D**)
- Piston Dish Volume (**P**) or Dome Volume (-**P**)
- Cylinder Volume (**V**)

When the piston is at BDC, the total volume is all of these volumes added together. When the piston is at TDC, the total volume is all of these EXCEPT the Cylinder Volume (V). So... true compression ratio is this:

$$\frac{V + D + G + C + P}{D + G + C + P}$$

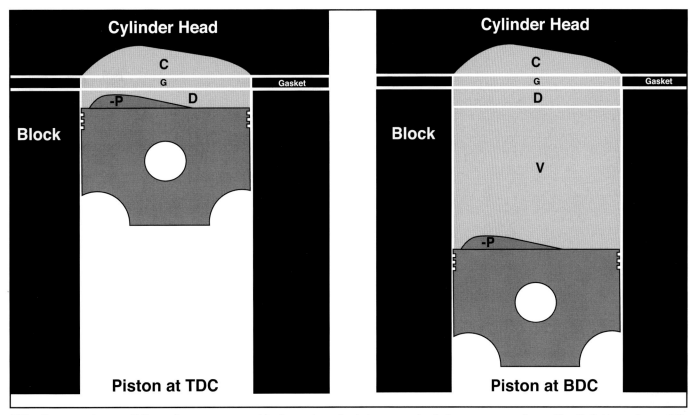

This diagram shows all the volumes you need to know to calculate an engine's true compression ratio: Cylinder volume (V), piston dome (-P) or dish volume (P), piston/deck height (D), compressed gasket volume (G), and the combustion chamber volume (C). The compression ratio is the volume of the cylinder and combustion chamber (V + P + D + G +C) when the piston is at bottom dead center, compared to the volume of the combustion chamber (P + D + G +C) when the piston is at top dead center.

Combustion Chamber Volume

Combustion chamber volumes for stock heads and aftermarket heads are typically available from the manufacturer. If you can't find the info or if you've modified the combustion chambers, you'll have to measure the volumes (using a plastic deck plate, burettes, and a graduated cylinder) or have your local machine shop do it for you.

Converting cc's to ci's

Combustion chamber volume, dome volume, and dish volume are generally measured in cc's, not cubic inches. To convert cc's to cubic inches, divide the measurement in cc's by 16.4.

$$cc/16.4 = ci$$

Compressed Head Gasket Volume

Compressed head gasket volume is simply the volume of the cylinder hole in the head gasket — think of it as a very shallow cylinder. So, its volume is computed the same way you compute cylinder volume:

B x B x Gasket Thickness x 0.7854 = Compressed Head Gasket Volume

In this case, the gasket's compressed thickness is .038 inches, so . . .

4.000" x 4.000" x .038" x 0.7854 = 0.4775232 ci

Piston/Deck Height Volume

Piston/Deck height volume is the small volume at the top of the cylinder that is not swept by the piston. Measure piston/deck height with a dial indicator. Bring the piston to top dead center (TDC) and measure the distance from the top of the piston to the deck of the block. This is normally somewhere between .008 and .025 inch. If the block deck has been machined, say .010 inch, then deck height will be smaller.

Once again, this volume is a shallow cylinder. Compute its volume by plugging the piston/deck height measurement (D) into the cylinder volume formula:

B x B x D x 0.7854 = Piston/Deck Height Volume

In our example, this measurement was .015 inch, so we plug in that value to compute piston/deck height volume in cubic inches.

4.000" x 4.000" x .015" x 0.7854 = 0.188496 ci

Piston Dome/Dish Volume

The last bit of information we need is the volume of the piston dome or dish (dish includes valve reliefs, too). Because the dishes or domes are irregularly shaped, it's necessary to either measure the volume using burettes and graduated cylinders, or you can usually get the measurement from the piston manufacturer. If the piston is domed, the dome reduces the amount of volume in the combustion chamber, so its volume is subtracted. If the piston is dished, the dish increases the volume of the combustion chamber, so its volume is added. In this example, our 302 has flat-top pistons with valve reliefs that measure 2 cc in volume. That 2 cc increases the cylinder volume, so we give it a positive value. If the pistons were domed, the dome would reduce the cylinder volume, so we'd give it a negative value. Either way, the volume has to be converted from cc's to ci's:

$$cc / 16.4 = ci$$
$$2\ cc / 16.4 = .121951\ ci$$

So, let's check the true compression ratio for that 302-ci engine, assuming it has a combustion chamber volume of 63 cc, a compressed head gasket thickness of .038 inch, and a piston/deck height of .015 inch. Here's what we've figured out so far:

V=Cylinder Volume: 37.6992 ci *(calculated)*
C=Combustion Chamber Volume: 63 cc (3.8414634 ci) *(measured)*
G=Compressed Head Gasket Volume: 0.4775232 ci *(calculated)*
P=Piston Dome Volume: .121951 ci *(measured)*
D=Piston/Deck Height Volume: 0.188496 ci *(calculated)*

Now (finally!) we're ready to calculate our true compression ratio, using the formula we developed earlier:

$$\frac{V + D + G + C + P}{D + G + C + P}$$

Plug in the values:

$$\frac{37.6992\ ci + 0.188496\ ci + 0.4775232\ ci + 3.8414634\ ci + .121951\ ci}{0.188496\ ci + 0.4775232\ ci + 3.8414634\ ci + .121951\ ci}$$

$$\frac{42.328634}{4.629434}$$

That gives us a true compression ratio, for this engine, of 9.1:1.

CHOOSING THE RIGHT CARBURETOR SIZE

Seems a lot of folks specify a larger carburetor than they actually need. Here's an easy formula that will put you on target every time, as long as you're honest with yourself about where your engine's going to operate. We want to look at cubic inches and the best volumetric efficiency (VE). With street engines, volumetric efficiency is typically around 75 to 80 percent. Boost the performance and VE goes up to 80 to 95 percent. The best indicator of engine performance is an engine dynamometer. This formula will calculate the required carb size for your engine:

$$\frac{VE\ (Volumetric\ Efficiency)\ x\ ci\ x\ Max\ RPMs}{3456}$$

For example, we've built a 302 that's performing strong on the dyno. The dyno figures tell us 85 percent VE. On the street, we figure the max RPM this engine will see is 5,500 rpm. So, if we plug in the numbers, we get:

$$\frac{.85\ x\ 302\ x\ 6,000}{3456}$$

Do the math, and we end up with 445.66 cfm. As you can see, there are probably a lot of engines running around with too much carburetor.

CALCULATING HORSEPOWER AND TORQUE

Horsepower and torque are words we hear a lot in the automotive realm. Which do you believe is more significant to power output? It may surprise you to learn that torque is the more significant number. Did you know horsepower and torque are the same at 5,252 rpm on any engine? That's because horsepower is derived from torque. Here's a good formula to remember:

$$Horsepower = \frac{RPM\ x\ Torque}{5,252\ rpm}$$

If you do a little cross-multiplying, you can also rearrange this equation to compute torque from horsepower:

$$Torque = \frac{5,252\ rpm\ x\ Horsepower}{RPM}$$

ESTIMATING HORSEPOWER AT THE DRAGS

Your car's approximate horsepower and torque can be determined with a simple quarter-mile pass at the drag strip. Begin by weighing your vehicle – you can find scales at a farm co-op (anyplace that sells grain or feed by the truckload) or truck weigh station along the interstate. Then make several quarter-mile passes and calculate an average top mph. Then make the following calculation:

$$Horsepower = \frac{Weight\ x\ 0.4\ x\ 1/4\text{-}mile\ MPH}{282}$$

Assume your car weighs 3,000 pounds, and your average quarter-mile time was 100 mph. Plug in the numbers and we get . . .

$$\frac{3000\ lbs\ x\ 0.4\ x\ 100\ mph}{282} = 425.53191\ hp$$

If you know what RPM your engine was turning as you went through the traps, you can also figure out the torque your engine generates. If we went through the traps at 6,000 rpm, we can calculate torque by doing the following formula:

$$\frac{5,252\ x\ 425\ Hp}{6000\ rpm} = 372\ ft\text{-}lbs.\ of\ torque$$

These calculations are approximate, but close enough to make a good guess at your engine's output.

SOURCE GUIDE

Automotive Racing Products (ARP)
1863 Eastman Ave.
Ventura, CA 93003
805/339-2200
www.arp-bolts.com

ACCEL Performance Products
Mr. Gasket Performance Group
10601 Memphis Ave. #12
Cleveland, OH 44144
216/688-8300
www.accel-ignition.com

Air Flow Research (AFR)
10490 Ilex Ave.
Pacoima, CA 91331-3137
818/890-0616
www.airflowresearch.com

Barry Grant Fuel Systems
1450 McDonald Rd.
Dahlonega, GA 30533
706/864-8544
www.barrygrant.com

Be Cool, Inc.
310 Woodside Ave.
Essexville, MI 48732
800/691-2667
989/895-9699
www.becool.com

Branda Mustang & Shelby
1434 E. Pleasant Valley Blvd.
Altoona, PA 16602
814/942-1869
www.cobranda.com

Brothers Performance Warehouse
2012 Railroad St.
Corona, CA 92880
800/486-2681
www.BrothersPerformance.com

Coast High Performance
2555 W. 237th St.
Torrance, CA 90505
310/784-1010
www.coasthigh.com

Comp Cams
3406 Democrat Rd.
Memphis, TN 38118
901/795-2400
www.compcams.com

Crane Cams
530 Fentress Ave.
Daytona Beach, FL 32114
386-252-1151
386/258-6174 (Tech Line)
www.cranecams.com

D&D Motorsports, Inc.
661/260-2226
661/260-2225 (FAX)
www.dndmotorsports.com

Edelbrock Corporation
2700 California St.
Torrance, CA 90503
310/781-2222
www.edelbrock.com

Flowmaster Mufflers
100 Stony Point Rd., #125
Santa Rosa, CA 95401
800/544-4761
www.flowmaster.com

Holley Performance Products
1801 Russellville Rd.
Bowling Green, KY 42102-7360
270/782-2900
270/781-9741 (Tech Line)
www.holley.com

Ignitioneering
2216 E. Mineral King
Visalia, CA 93292
559/739-1515
www.ignitioneering.com

JBA
7149 Mission Gorge Rd., Suite D
San Diego, CA 92120
800/830-3377
www.jbaheaders.com

K&N Performance
P.O. Box 1329
Riverside, CA 92502
888/949-1832
www.knfilters.com

Mallory Ignition
Mr. Gasket Performance Group
10601 Memphis Ave.
Cleveland, OH 44144
216/688-8300
www.mrgasket.com

MSD Ignition
1490 Henry Brennan Dr.
El Paso, TX 79936
915/857-5200
www.msdignition.com

Mustangs Plus
2353 N. Wilson Way
Stockton, CA 95205
800/999-4289
209/994-9977
www.mustangsplus.com

Mustangs Unlimited
185 Adams St.
Manchester, CT 06040
860/647-1965
860/649-1260 (FAX)
www.mustangsunlimited.com

Performance Distributors
2899 Barris Dr.
Memphis, TN 38132
901/396-5782
www.performancedistributors.com

Performance Parts, Inc.
13120 Lazy Glen Ct.
Oak Hill, VA 20171-2326
703/742-6207
www.mustangparts.com

Saleen Autosports
76 Fairbanks
Irvine, CA 92618
800/888-8945
949/597-4900
949/597-4917 (FAX)
www.saleen.com

Steeda Autosports
1351 NW Steeda Way
Pompano Beach, FL 33069
954/960-0774
www.steeda.com

USA Racing
2340 W. Pioneer Pkwy.
Arlington, TX 76013
877/695-RACE
817/461-6066
817/461-1442 (FAX)
www.usamotorsportsinc.com

WORKBENCH
REFERENCE CHARTS

Recommended Maximum Torque for General Automotive Applications (in ft-lbs)

See the table below for specific bolt torque recommendations

U.S. Standards for Bolt Dimensions				Grade: SAE 2 Tensile: 74,000		Grade: SAE 5 Tensile: 120,000		Grade: SAE 7 Tensile: 133,000		Grade: SAE 8 Tensile: 150,000		Special Alloys 180,000+	ARP** Tensile 170,000	ARP** Tensile 190,000
Bolt Diameter (in.)	Threads per inch	Decimal Equivalent	Bolt Head	Dry	Lubed	Dry	Lubed	Dry	Lubed	Dry	Lubed	Lubed with Washers	With ARP Lube	With ARP Lube
1/4 stud	20/28	.250	–	–	–	–	–	–	–	–	–	14	8	9
1/4	20	.250	7/16	5.5	4	8	6	10	8	10	8	12	9	10
1/4	28	.250	7/16	6	4.5	10	7	12	9	14	10	15	10	11
5/16 stud	18/24	.3125	–	–	–	–	–	–	–	–	–	30	18	19
5/16	18	.3125	1/2	11	8	17	13	21	16	25	18	26	19	21
5/16	24	.3125	1/2	12	9	19	14	24	18	25	20	26	20	22
3/8 stud	16/24	.375	–	–	–	–	–	–	–	–	–	60	30	40
3/8	16	.375	9/16	20	15	30	23	40	30	45	35	36	33	36
3/8	24	.375	9/16	23	17	35	25	45	30	50	35	38	35	38
7/16 stud	14/20	.4375	–	–	–	–	–	–	–	–	–	83	50	65
7/16	14	.4375	5/8	32	24	50	35	60	45	70	55	61	57	62
7/16	20	.4375	5/8	36	27	55	40	70	50	80	60	67	58	63
1/2 stud	13/20	.500	–	–	–	–	–	–	–	–	–	130	76	83
1/2	13	.500	3/4	50	35	75	55	95	70	110	80	105	84	92
1/2	20	.500	3/4	55	40	90	65	100	80	120	90	110	89	97
9/16 stud	12/18	.5625	–	–	–	–	–	–	–	–	–	181	n/a	115
9/16	12	.5625	7/8	70	55	110	80	135	100	150	110	155	116	127
9/16	18	.5625	7/8	80	60	120	90	150	110	170	130	175	121	132
5/8	11	.625	15/16	100	75	150	110	190	140	220	170	215	160	175
5/8	18	.625	15/16	110	85	180	130	210	160	240	180	250	172	188
3/4	10	.750	1-1/8	175	130	260	200	320	240	380	280	340	–	–
3/4	16	.750	1-1/8	200	150	300	220	360	280	420	320	380	–	–

Tables Provided Courtesy of Automotive Racing Products (ARP).

Size	Bolt Head	Usage	Recommended Torque (ft-lbs)
1/4-20	7/16	Timing chain cover	7
		Oil pan to crankcase	6
		Oil filter bypass valve	7
		Oil pump cover	7
		Rockerarm cover	4
5/16-18	1/2	Camshaft sprocket	20
		Oil pan to crankcase	9
		Oil filter bypass valve	14
3/8-16	9/16	Clutch pressure plate	35
		Distributor clamp	20
		Exhaust manifold	20
		Exhaust manifold (inside bolts on V-8 engines	30
		Intake manifold	32
		Manifold water outlet	30
		Water pump	30
		Lower pulley	30
3/8-24	9/16	Connecting rod	45
7/16-14	5/8	Cylinder head	65
		Main bearing cap	75
		Main bearing cap (outer bolts, with 4-bolt caps)	65
		Oil pump	65
		Rockerarm stud	50
7/16-20	5/8	Flywheel	60
		Damper	60
1/2-14	3/4	Temperature send unit	20
1/2-20	3/4	Oil filter	25
		Oil pan drain plug	20
14 mm and 5/8		Sparkplug	25

Thread Sizes and Tap Drills

Thread Size	Major Diameter (inch)	Root Diameter (inch)	Tap Drill to Produce 75% of Full Thread	Tap Drill Decimal Equivalent (inch)
6-32	.1380	.0974	36	.1065
6-40	.1380	.1055	33	.1130
8-32	.1640	.1234	29	.1360
8-36	.1640	.1279	29	.1360
10-24	.1900	.1359	25	.1495
10-32	.1900	.1494	21	.1590
12-24	.2160	.1619	16	.1770
12-28	.2160	.1696	14	.1820
1/4-20	.2500	.1850	7	.2010
1/4-28	.2500	.2036	3	.2130
5/16-18	.3125	.2403	F	.2570
5/16-24	.3125	.2584	I	.2720
3/8-16	.3750	.2938	5/16	.3125
3/8-24	.3750	.3209	Q	.3320
7/16-14	.4735	.3447	U	.3580
7/16-20	.4375	.3726	25/64	.3906
1/2-13	.5000	.4001	27/64	.4219
1/2-20	.5000	.4351	29/64	.4531
9/16-12	.5625	.4542	31/64	.4844
9/16-18	.5625	.4903	33/64	.5156
5/8-11	.6250	.5069	17/32	.5312
5/8-18	.6250	.5528	37/64	.5781
3/4-10	.7500	.6201	21/32	.6562
3/4-16	.7500	.6688	11/16	.6875

Unless otherwise indicated, the torque specifications given on this page are for lubricated fasteners. While you can install fasteners dry, you will find that lubrication allows fasteners to screw in easier, prevents thread seizure, and gives more accurate torque readings. If you decide to use lubrication, use Vaseline or petrolatum. To compensate for lubrication, torque values are often reduced by about 10 to 25 percent. This reduction may not be required for the small (under 1/4 inch), high-quality fasteners.

S-A Design *Work-A-Long Sheet*®

DISASSEMBLY

Project Statistics
Your Name _____

Today's Date _____ Vehicle Engine Removed From _____

Engine Year _____ CI _____ Block Casting _____ ☐ 2 barrel ☐ 4 barrel ☐ Fuel Injection

Accessories Attached to Used Engine
☐ A/C Pump ☐ AIR Pump ☐ AIR Distributor Lines and Hoses ☐ Water Pump
☐ Flywheel ☐ Clutch ☐ Flexplate ☐ Transmission
☐ Starter ☐ Fuel Pump ☐ Exhaust Manifolds ☐ All Pulleys; Except _____
☐ Alternator ☐ Distributor ☐ Coil ☐ Carburetor
☐ Motor Mounts ☐ Motor Mount Attaching Brackets ☐ Spark Plug Heat Shields
☐ EGR Valve ☐ Dipstick Tube ☐ All Bolts; except _____
☐ _____ ☐ _____ ☐ _____ ☐ _____ ☐ _____

Operational Notes
Oil consumption _____ Compression check pressure variation _____ psi

Leak-down percent _____ Other observations _____

Disassembly Notations
Crank uses centerbolt ☐ Yes ☐ No

Heat riser restricted on ☐ Left ☐ Right ☐ Both

Head gaskets ☐ Steel shim ☐ Composition

Worn/damaged lifters ☐ No ☐ Yes; where _____

Vibration damper pulley screws ☐ 3/8-NC ☐ 3/8-NF

Location of timing-pointer attaching points:

Oil filter adapter type:
☐ Spin-on
☐ Long cartridge (late)
☐ Short cartridge (early)

Type of rear main seal:
☐ Rubber—two piece
☐ Rubber—one piece (late)
☐ Rope (early)

INSPECTION

Initial Parts Inspection Observations
Block OK ☐ Yes ☐ No; describe problem _____
Heads OK ☐ Yes ☐ No; describe problem _____
Crank Ok ☐ Yes ☐ No; describe problem _____
Bearings OK ☐ Yes ☐ No; describe problem _____
Pistons OK ☐ Yes ☐ No; describe problem _____
Cam/lifters OK ☐ Yes ☐ No; describe problem _____
Damper OK ☐ Yes ☐ No; describe problem _____
Intake manifold OK ☐ Yes ☐ No; describe problem _____
Exhaust manifold OK ☐ Yes ☐ No; describe problem _____
Oil pump OK ☐ Yes ☐ No; describe problem _____

Oil pump/rear main cap mating surfaces damage/abnormalities ☐ No ☐ Yes

Identifying mark you placed on all parts:

_____

AT THE MACHINE SHOP

Parts Delivered to the Machine Shop

☐ Block ☐ Main Caps ☐ Crankshaft ☐ Oil Pump ☐ Oil Pump Pickup
☐ Connecting Rods ☐ Pistons ☐ Piston Rings ☐ Camshaft ☐ Lifters
☐ Vibration Damper ☐ Main Bearings ☐ Rod Bearings ☐ Cam Bearings ☐ Rod Bolts
☐ Gasket Set ☐ Push Rods ☐ Rockerarms ☐ Head Bolts ☐ Main Bolts/Studs
☐ Miscellaneous Nuts/Bolts/Brackets for Cleaning ☐ _____
☐ Water Pump ☐ Timing Cover ☐ Oil Pan ☐ Flywheel/Flexplate
☐ Clutch ☐ Exhaust Manifolds ☐ Motor Mounts ☐ Motor Mount Attaching Brackets
☐ Assembled Heads ☐ Disassembled Heads with: ☐ Valves ☐ Springs ☐ Retainers ☐ Keepers
  ☐ Rocker Balls and Nuts ☐
☐ Intake Manifold ☐ With Heat Riser Shield ☐ Installed ☐ Not Installed
☐ _____ ☐ _____ ☐ _____ ☐ _____ ☐ _____
☐ _____ ☐ _____ ☐ _____ ☐ _____ ☐ _____
☐ _____ ☐ _____ ☐ _____ ☐ _____ ☐ _____
☐ Other Accessories _____

Special Instructions for Machine Shop

☐ Bore block ☐ Use torque plates ☐ Desired piston-to-wall clearance: O. _____ -inch
☐ Grind crank ☐ Rod bearing clearance: O. _____ -inch ☐ Main bearing clearance: O. _____ -inch
☐ Deck to clean ☐ Surface heads ☐ Install cam bearings ☐ _____
☐ _____ ☐ _____ ☐ _____
☐ _____ ☐ _____

Is pilot bushing to be installed in crankshaft (required for manual transmission)? ☐ Yes ☐ No
Are intake manifold heat shield holes to be tapped for 8-32 screws? ☐ Yes ☐ No

After You Pick Up Your Parts

☐ Yes ☐ No Threaded holes reconditioned/chased ☐ Yes ☐ No Drilled holes and edges chamfered
☐ Yes ☐ No head/block dowels properly installed ☐ Yes ☐ No Are cam bearings properly installed
☐ Yes ☐ No Galleries tapped for screw-in plugs ☐ Yes ☐ No Add 0.030-inch hole in gallery plug
☐ Yes ☐ No Add 0.030-inch hole in thrust face ☐ Yes ☐ No Core plugs properly installed
☐ Yes ☐ No Retaining straps on core plugs ☐ Yes ☐ No Crank keys properly installed
☐ Yes ☐ No Manifold heat-shield holes tapped for 8-32 screws

PRE-ASSEMBLY FITTING

Measured and Recorded During Pre-Assembly Fitting

☐ Yes ☐ No Do all valveguides have proper clearance? If no, which are correct _____
☐ Yes ☐ No Do all valveseats meet dimensional specs? If no, which are faulty _____
☐ Yes ☐ No Do all valveseats hold solvent? If no, which leak _____
☐ Yes ☐ No Have all valveguides been machined concentric for press-on seals?

Retainer to Valveguide clearance O. _____ -inch; adequate on all valves? ☐ Yes ☐ No If no, which valves have
  insufficient clearance? _____

Recommended valvespring seat pressure _____ psi at _____ -inches installed height.

Measured valvespring installed height:

1 _____ 3 _____ 5 _____ 7 _____
2 _____ 4 _____ 6 _____ 8 _____

Spring shims used to obtain correct installed height:

1 _____ 3 _____ 5 _____ 7 _____
2 _____ 4 _____ 6 _____ 8 _____

Measured valvespring solid height _____-inches
Calculated compressed spring clearance:

1 _____ 3 _____ 5 _____ 7 _____
2 _____ 4 _____ 6 _____ 8 _____

Connecting rod bore OK? ☐ Yes ☐ No; Which rods are defective _____
Crank straightness OK? ☐ Yes ☐ No Runout on center main of 0._____-inch
Main bearing clearance OK? ☐ Yes ☐ No Measured clearance 0. _____-inch
Crank thrust OK? ☐ Yes ☐ No Measured clearance 0. _____-inch
Main bearing clearance OK? ☐ Yes ☐ No Measured clearance 0. _____-inch
Camshaft bearing fit OK? ☐ Yes ☐ No; Describe problem _____
Block required clearance grinding for upper sprocket? ☐ Yes ☐ No
Pin end clearance OK? ☐ Yes ☐ No Measured clearance 0. _____-inch
Piston-to-wall clearance OK? ☐ Yes ☐ No Measured clearance 0. _____-inch
Pistons with incorrect clearance _____

Measured ring end gap:

1 Top _____ 2nd _____ 3 Top _____ 2nd _____ 5 Top _____ 2nd _____ 7 Top _____ 2nd _____
2 Top _____ 2nd _____ 4 Top _____ 2nd _____ 6 Top _____ 2nd _____ 8 Top _____ 2nd _____

Rod bearing clearance OK? ☐ Yes ☐ No Measured clearance 0. _____-inch
Rod side clearance OK? ☐ Yes ☐ No Measured clearance 0. _____-inch
Piston-to-head clearance OK? ☐ Yes ☐ No Measured clearance 0. _____-inch
Cylinders with incorrect clearance _____
Offset bushings/key used: ☐ + – 2° ☐ + – 4° ☐ + – 6° ☐ + – 8° ☐ + – 10° ☐ + – 12°

Rotating assembly clearance OK? ☐ Yes ☐ No; Cause of interference _____
Crank index OK? ☐ Yes ☐ No Maximum _____° out of index on journal no. _____
Cylinder-to-cylinder deck height accurate? ☐ Yes ☐ No Maximum 0. _____-inch variation.
Rocker geometry OK? ☐ Yes ☐ No; Describe problem _____
Rocker-to-stud clearance OK? ☐ Yes ☐ No Maximum 0. _____-inch (Intake); 0. _____-inch (Exhaust);
Piston-to-valve clearance OK? ☐ Yes ☐ No Maximum 0. _____-inch (Intake); 0. _____-inch (Exhaust);
Oil pump drive clearance OK? ☐ Yes ☐ No Measured clearance 0. _____-inch
Intake manifold end-rail clearance OK? ☐ Yes ☐ No Measured clearance 0. _____-inch
Manifold surface parallel with head? ☐ Yes ☐ No; Describe problem _____
Pulleys/accessories aligned? ☐ Yes ☐ No; Describe problem _____

_____
_____